THE FINAL WORD

*A Biblical Response to the Case
for Tongues and Prophecy Today*

*

O. Palmer Robertson

THE BANNER OF TRUTH TRUST

THE BANNER OF TRUTH TRUST
3 Murrayfield Road, Edinburgh EH12 6EL
P.O. Box 621, Carlisle, Pennsylvania 17013, USA

*

© O. Palmer Robertson 1993
First Published 1993
Reprinted 1997
Reprinted 2004
ISBN 0 85151 659 9

*

Typeset in 10½/12pt Plantin Monotype
Printed and bound in Great Britain by
Bell & Bain Ltd., Glasgow

Contents

Chapter One

Prophecy Today?

1. THE ORIGIN OF PROPHECY ACCORDING TO THE OLD TESTAMENT

Biblical prophecy had its origins in the Old Testament, which is a fact of some significance. Prophecy is not a distinctly New Testament phenomenon, but one which dates back to the most ancient experiences of God's people. But when and where did prophecy first arise? Surprisingly, prophecy did not have its origins in the age of the great eighth-century B.C. figures such as Isaiah, Micah and Hosea. Instead, prophecy began in a much more ancient setting.

Moses was the fountainhead of the prophetic movement in the Old Testament. As a matter of fact, Old Testament prophecy reached its point of highest glory with Moses. Contrary to all concepts of an evolutionary development of religion in Israel, the apex of the prophetic movement found its expression in Moses, the original prophet and law-giver in Israel. He played a unique role as mediator of the word of God to the people of Israel.

In the days before Moses, God spoke personally to the heads of the various patriarchal families. The fatherly head

1

THE FINAL WORD

would then communicate the word of God to his clan. But how was God to communicate his word to a host of over a million people as they came out of Egypt? Would the Lord reveal himself simultaneously to 600,000 heads of families? Or would he continue throughout the subsequent ages of Israel's history to thunder with his own voice from heaven as he did at Sinai?

God's people themselves had strong feelings on this matter. They pleaded with Moses: give us a substitute for this terrifying experience of hearing the thunder of God's voice (*Deut.* 18:16). In response to the plea of the people, God provided a prophetic mediator and established the prophetic office. One man would receive the word of God in the mountain and subsequently mediate the word to the trembling people below. In this way prophecy had its origins.

Several significant conclusions may be reached about the nature of biblical prophecy as a consequence of the circumstances surrounding its establishment. The origins of prophecy reveal matters of continuing significance about the essence of the phenomenon.

a. *The small, simple voice of the prophet substitutes for all the awesome signs of Sinai.* The thunderous voice of God, the lightning, the fire, the smoke, the earthquake, the peal of the trumpet growing ever louder — all these frightening phenomena find their replacement in the voice of a single Israelite speaking among his brothers. Despite its relatively quiet tone, every word of the prophet comes as the very voice of God.

b. *The origin of the truly prophetic word is not to be found in the subjective experiences of a man.* The prophet is not hallucinating when he declares, 'Thus says the Lord.' God's own word has come to the prophet, and its vehicle of communication is the chosen man's voice. God, not the subjective experiences of man, originates the prophetic word.

c. *The word of the prophet is not primarily predictive in nature.*
Moses' main task in delivering the law at Sinai was not to predict the future, but to declare God's revealed will. Not a single prediction is found in the 'ten words', the heart of the revelation communicated through Moses.

The common distinction between the 'forth-telling' of the prophetic word and the 'fore-telling' of the future by the prophet must be understood correctly. From the beginning, the 'telling forth' of God's word was just as much a revelation of the infallible, inerrant and perfect word of God as was his 'fore-telling' of the future. It simply is not the case that the speaking forth of the prophet on various issues of the day was a kind of 'preaching' with diminished authority, while his 'fore-telling' of the future was inspired, inerrant and infallible in its character.

As a matter of fact, the essence of prophetism is always defined in the Bible in terms of this 'speaking forth' of the very word of God, whether or not it involved a foretelling of the future. Occasionally the prophet might predict a future event. Obviously, this kind of insight could occur only by divine revelation. But the essence of prophecy was not determined by the predictive element, but by the nature of the prophet's utterance as being the very word of God.

Geerhardus Vos addresses this subject in his article on 'The Idea of "Fulfilment" of Prophecy in the Gospels'. With respect to the nature of prophecy, he says:

> In connection with the foregoing [the idea of the fulfilment of prophecy], the question may be raised, What is precisely the force of the 'pro' in the name 'prophet'? Does 'prophet' mean 'foreteller' or does it

3

> mean 'forthteller', i.e. 'the one who speaks forth a word
> revealed to him by God'? In the Hebrew *nabhi* the latter
> finds expression, and it is, so to speak, an unexpressed
> circumstance that the word forthspoken in many cases
> happens to be a 'prediction'. [1]

Prophecy should not be defined essentially as a foretelling of the future. Instead, it is the forthtelling of a revelation from God which on occasion also may involve the prediction of future events.

This perspective on the essence of prophecy is important for evaluating the question of the continuation of prophecy today. Obviously, no one can foretell infallibly the specifics of a future event, as was the case in biblical prophecy, unless one has experienced a direct revelation from God. But it is equally true that no one can 'tell forth' the word of God in the prophetic sense apart from experiencing a direct revelation from God. Whether as 'fore-teller' or 'forth-teller', the prophet communicated revelation from God. If a person affirms that biblical prophecy continues today in either of its basic forms, it should be clear that he is expressing belief that revelation continues today. While a contemporary preacher may be 'prophetic' in his pulpit ministry, he is not 'prophesying' in the biblical sense as seen in the history of the origins of prophetism.

d. A further conclusion may be reached with respect to the nature of prophecy on the basis of its origins as preserved in Scripture. *The ultimate goal of God's covenant cannot be realised so long as a prophetic figure must stand between the Lord and his people.*

God's purpose in the covenant was to be one with his people. In establishing a covenant relationship, the Lord binds himself intimately to his people. But that closeness of relationship which God intended by the covenant cannot be achieved so long as a prophetic mediator must stand between God and the people. So long as a mediator must run from the top of the mountain to the people below, covenantal unity has not been fully realised.

This point is emphasised by Paul in his statement that 'a mediator does not speak of one' (*Gal.* 3:20). The presence of a mediator implicitly suggests a separation of people from one another. Only if God himself should become the one who mediates the divine word could the oneness of fellowship intended by the covenant be fulfilled. Then the need for the intermediary work of the prophetic figure would come to an end.

This perspective on the final goal of prophetism is confirmed by the testimony of the new covenant documents. The writer to the Hebrews speaks of the finality of the prophetic revelation as it is found in Jesus Christ. Previously God spoke in many different ways through many different prophetic mediators. But now he has spoken with finality in a Son (*Heb.* 1:1). When the prophetic revelation comes directly through Jesus Christ, then the ultimate goal of the covenant has been realised. Experiencing the revelation of God through the Son means being one with God himself.

2. FOUNDATIONAL PASSAGES ON PROPHECY IN THE OLD TESTAMENT

The historical context of the origin of prophetism in Israel provides a firm foundation for understanding the true nature of prophecy as it is manifest in subsequent history. This understanding finds significant elucidation in several other foundational passages on prophecy in the Old Testament. Essential to an appreciation of the role of prophetism in the new covenant is this old covenant background. Let us consider the following passages:

a. *Exodus 7:1-2*: 'Then the Lord said to Moses, See, I have made you like God to Pharaoh, and your brother Aaron will be your prophet. You are to say everything I command you, and your brother Aaron is to tell Pharaoh to let the Israelites go out of his country' (NIV).

In this passage Moses is as God, Aaron is his prophet and Pharaoh is the recipient of the prophetic word. Though the word of God originating with Moses is mediated through Aaron, it comes to Pharaoh with un-diminished authority. Pharaoh's land is devastated because he does not heed the infallible, inerrant word of God communicated through Aaron who serves as Moses' 'prophet'. Mediatorship in no way diminishes the authority of the prophetic word.

b. *Exodus 4:15-16*: 'Now you shall speak to him and put the words in his mouth. And I will be with your mouth and with his mouth, and I will teach you what you shall do. So he (that is, Aaron as prophet for Moses) shall be your spokesman to the people. And he himself shall be as a mouth for you, and you shall be to him as God' (NKJV).

'Mouth to mouth': the descriptive phrase underscores the immediacy of the relationship that exists between God's Word and the prophetic word. The divine revelation goes directly from the mouth of God to the mouth of the prophet. The word of the prophet is the very Word of God. God does not communicate his revelation to the prophet 'thought to thought' or 'mind to mind', but 'mouth to mouth'. Prophetism, by definition, is concerned not merely with the reception of the Word of God, but with its communication as well. This description of the mode of communication of the prophetic word under-scores the absolute perfections of the prophet's speech in representing God's Word. By a 'mouth to mouth' communication, God's Word is preserved in its integrity as it passes through the vehicle of the prophet.

c. *Numbers 12:6-7*: God said, 'Listen to my words: When a prophet of the Lord is among you, in a vision unto him I shall make myself known; in a dream to him I shall speak.'

The prophetic parallelism of the original text underscores the revelatory character of the message that comes to the prophet:

a In a vision
    b unto him
        c I shall make myself known;

a In a dream
    b to him
        c I shall speak.

God will take the initiative in making himself known by vision and dream. This mode of divine communication will characterize the experience of the prophet through the ages. The 'vision' and the 'dream' of the prophet originate with God, not with the insight of man. Although the context indicates that distinctive favour will be shown to Moses in that God will speak to him 'face to face', there can be no discounting of the fact that all the prophets will receive their message by a revelatory experience. That is the meaning of the Word's coming through 'dream' and 'vision'.

Strikingly suitable to this idea of prophetic revelation that comes through 'dream' and 'vision' is the fact that written prophecy in the Old Testament is presented vividly as a thing 'seen'. The writings of Isaiah the prophet are described as a 'vision' (*hazon*) which he 'saw' (*haza*). Subsequently, the 'word' (*hadaver*) which Isaiah 'saw' (*haza*) describes a particular message he received (*Isa.* 2:1).

The prophets experienced this form of revelation

repeatedly. Isaiah 'saw' the Lord's 'burden' (*Isa.* 13:1).
Amos and Micah 'saw' their word from the Lord (*Amos*
1:1, *Mic.* 1:1). Habakkuk speaks of his entire book as a
'burden' that he 'saw' (*Hab.* 1:1). The prophets regularly
'saw' through 'vision' and 'dream' the word they were to
communicate.

In contrast with this visionary reception of God's Word by
a revelatory experience, the false prophets speak out of their
own hearts. Jeremiah vivifies the major characteristic of the
origin of the word of the false prophets. He declares: 'A
vision from their heart they speak, not from the mouth of
the Lord' (*Jer.* 23:16). The word of the false prophet
originates with the machinations of his own heart, not with
the visionary experience granted to the true prophet of
the Lord.

d. This contrast between true and false prophets is continued in the fourth foundational passage: *Deuteronomy
13:4-5*. Rather than heeding the false prophet who originates his own dreams, Israel must keep God's commands as
delivered by his prophets. God's nation must observe the
way God commanded it to go. The false prophet 'must be
put to death' because he has attempted to turn Israel from
the revealed way it must follow.

Over against the deliverances of the false prophets are set
the commands, ordinances and statutes that have been
revealed through Moses and his true successors. The most
basic test of the prophet is his adherence to the 'forth-
telling' that already has come by divine revelation.

The prophets were not primarily predictors. No matter
how spectacular a prophet's words might appear, he must
be put to death if his statements contradicted the rather
non-spectacular commands revealed to Moses, the prophet
par excellence.

This respect for the divine character of the prophetic

word needs to be carried over into the context of the new covenant. As we shall see, the denigration of prophecy to the level of non-revelational or semi-revelational 'forth-telling' finds no encouragement in the foundational texts on prophecy in Scripture. Prophecy is a speaking forth of the revelatory word of God, whether his word predicts the future or declares God's commands. Prophecy in its most basic form is a 'forth-telling' of the *revelatory* truth of God. Prediction of the future indeed will occur, but it functions secondarily to the essence of prophecy.

e. The fifth foundational passage on prophecy is found in *Deuteronomy 18.* This passage reads like a section from a Hebrew version of *Roget's Thesaurus.* Every possible word describing a method by which men might attempt to determine, control or predict the future is designated as an abomination to the Lord. Any proposed substitution for the revelatory word of God that comes through his prophet must be utterly rejected.

In today's pluralist society, people find it almost impossible to express a categorical 'no' to any form of speaking or experience promoted in a devotional atmosphere by Christians. But God's word says 'no'. An unyielding resistance is required of the people of God with respect to any proposed substitutions for the divinely inspired prophetic word. In this case, God's people must speak with an absolute 'no'. No exception shall be allowed. Every form of non-biblical prophecy must be roundly condemned. Any effort to substitute man's fallible word for the divinely inspired prophetic word must be rejected.

This passage further declares that in the future a 'prophet' like Moses shall arise. This expectation anticipates in part the long history of prophetism in Israel that developed after Moses. In response to the continuous stream of false prophets that would develop in history, the Lord would raise up true prophets to answer their false counterparts.

Yet the text in Deuteronomy also seems to point to a singular prophetic figure that shall resemble Moses in a distinctive way. The passage does not say, 'Prophets the Lord your God shall raise up to you.' Instead, it states: 'a prophet like me the Lord your God shall raise up' (*Deut.* 18:15).

Israel's experience under Moses cries out for one who will come who is greater than Moses. If the purpose of God's covenant actually is to be fulfilled, then a prophetic mediator must come who in his person is more than Moses. Significant as the ministry of Moses might have been, it did not achieve the oneness between God and people that the covenant was intended to realise.

The prophet like Moses anticipated in this passage would speak the word of God with a power that would climax the shadowy form of Moses' revelations. Like Moses and his successors, this coming prophet may be rejected by the people. Yet because of the certainties of the covenant, he will succeed in his prophetic ministry where the original Moses failed.

In this light, it is not surprising to find the apostle Peter applying this passage from Deuteronomy 18:15 directly to Jesus in the book of Acts. Jesus is the 'servant' (*pais*) who is like Moses in that he mediates the word of God (*Acts* 3: 22, 26). But he is also the 'Son' of God (*pais* as well) who unites God with his people in fulfilment of the word of the covenant mediated through the prophets. If the Son of God himself now is the prophetic mediator of the covenant, then the ultimate goal of the covenant has been realised. Because to receive the word of God from the Son is to receive the word of God from the Lord himself. Now that through Christ the prophetic mediator of the covenant is himself the God of the covenant, the oneness between God and his people originally intended in the covenant has been established. Now the office of prophet will find its final realisation in this one person who is the Son of God and also the prophetic mediator of the covenant. Through his person, all the terrors related to the confrontation with God at Sinai are now removed. The fearsomeness once associated with standing in the presence of God evaporates when the mediator of the covenant is God himself, now standing among men as their servant (*pais*).

The history of kingship in Israel found its climax in Christ the king. The history of priesthood in Israel found its climax in Christ the priest. So also the history of prophetism in Israel finds its climax in Christ the prophet. He is the promised mediator *par excellence*. The Old Testament experience of a series of men who spoke God's very words finds its fulfilment in Jesus Christ, the prophet like Moses, who also excelled him in every way.

3. PROPHECY ABOUT PROPHECY IN THE OLD TESTAMENT

Having considered the testimony of these foundational passages about prophecy, it is now appropriate to consider a central Old Testament passage that has significance for understanding the phenomenon of prophecy as it appears in the New Testament. The classic 'prophecy about prophecy' in Joel 2 links the Old Testament experience with the New Testament phenomenon.

The word of God through Joel declares: 'I will pour out my Spirit on all flesh, and your sons and daughters shall prophesy' (*Joel* 2:28a, NKJV). In anticipating the future, Joel uses the identical term for 'prophecy' found throughout the rest of the Old Testament. Does this word suddenly have a new meaning? Is Joel expecting a different kind of prophecy from that described in the foundational passages already considered? No. Joel himself elaborates on the significance of his prediction: 'Your old men shall dream dreams, and your young men shall see visions' (*Joel* 2:28b).

Where did Joel get the idea that the prophetic word would be communicated through 'dream' and 'vision'? Was he the inventor of these concepts? No. Joel draws on the passage in Numbers 12 which so clearly describes the origin of prophetism in the days of Moses. Joel's terms for 'dreaming dreams' and 'seeing visions' are identical with the words used in Numbers 12 to describe the communication of revelation throughout the ages. Joel's language also parallels the description of the 'seeing' of a 'vision' that frequently serves as the heading of a divinely inspired prophetic book.

So what did Joel expect? What would be the experience of God's people with respect to prophecy in the future? Joel predicted a widespread manifestation of prophetic revelation in the future. The consummation of the ages would be accompanied by extensive revelatory experiences. Appropriate to the glory of Messiah's coming would be an unprecedented outpouring of the Holy Spirit, bringing with it many new revelations from God. Old men would 'dream dreams' and young men would 'see visions'. Both phrases describe experiences of a revelatory nature, drawing on the context of Numbers 12.

The New Testament indicates the fulfilment of this 'prophecy about prophecy' in several passages. Quoting Joel, Peter declares that the Old Testament prediction was fulfilled at the pouring out of the Spirit of prophecy at Pentecost (*Acts* 2:16). At this point, young men 'see visions' and old men 'dream dreams'. The Spirit's outpouring on the disciples at Pentecost did not cause them to hallucinate. They are not conjuring up religious ideas in the tradition of the false prophets. Neither are they achieving new levels of human insight. Instead, they are undergoing revelatory experiences. The language used repeatedly throughout the Old Testament period now applies to the prophets in a new covenant context.

This same understanding of prophecy continues throughout the book of Acts. In Acts 11:27-28 some 'prophets' came down from Jerusalem to Antioch. One of them named Agabus 'predicted through the Spirit' future events. The term translated 'predicted' literally means 'gave a sign'. This terminology further relates the experience of Agabus to the communication of revelation. Agabus' prophecy immediately became the basis for concrete action on the part of the disciples at Antioch. He revealed that a severe famine would spread over the entire Roman world. Recognising the distress this foreseen famine would bring on the disciples already suffering in Judea, the disciples at Antioch decided to provide help by sending a gift to the elders through Barnabas and Saul (*Acts* 11:29-30).

Clearly this experience of the new covenant prophet fits the Old Testament pattern. Agabus issued his prediction as the result of a revelational experience. By no other means could he have known of the development of a famine in the future other than by a direct revelation from God.

The phenomenon of prophecy in a new covenant context appears once more in Acts 21:8-11. Paul and Luke are staying at the house of Philip the evangelist, who is said to have 'four unmarried daughters who had the gift of prophecy' (verse 8). It should be remembered that Paul, who by this experience knew first-hand of the gift of prophecy as it was possessed by the four daughters of Philip, later gave approval to a woman's 'prophesying' in the church (*1 Cor.* 11:15).

But what is the nature of this 'prophesying' as done by the daughters of Philip? The verses immediately following clarify the question. The prophet Agabus comes down from

Judea and speaks revelationally by the power of the Holy Spirit. He predicts that Paul will be arrested in Jerusalem, which of course no one could know apart from a revelatory communication from God. Once more it becomes clear that the idea of 'prophet' in the New Testament is the same as the idea of 'prophet' in the Old Testament. Only by a direct revelation from God could Agabus have known that Paul was going to be arrested in Jerusalem.

It is in this context that the role of women as 'prophetesses' in the New Testament church should be considered. A woman might be regarded as a 'prophetess' if she functioned as an instrument of divine revelation. If revelation were continuing today, then it might be expected that women as well as men might legitimately 'prophesy' in the church today. We shall return to that point later.

These references to prophecy in Acts provide testimony concerning the actual experiences of both Peter and Paul with the gift of prophecy in a new covenant context. As such they provide a natural backdrop for the explicit treatment of the subject of prophecy by these two key apostles.

4. THE TESTIMONY OF PETER AND PAUL CONCERNING PROPHECY

Peter explicitly discusses prophecy in the last of his writings. He recognises the significance of his remarks, as the introductory phrase indicates: 'Know this first,' he says (2 Pet. 1:20-21). He intends to discuss a matter of great importance.

Peter here declares that 'no prophecy of Scripture came about by the prophet's own interpretation' (NIV). The prophetic word communicates truth from God that otherwise could not be known. The insight of man could not originate this understanding of the will of God. 'For prophecy never had its origin by the will of man, but men spoke from God as they were carried along by the Holy Spirit' (*2 Pet.* 1:21).

Peter does not treat prophecy as though it were equivalent to keenness of insight. Instead, he describes the experience of divine revelation. According to Peter all truly prophetic experiences partook of this same character. There is no exception. No true prophecy came 'by the will of man'. All true prophecy came by the revelation of God's Spirit. More particularly, Peter identifies this revelational experience with the words that the prophets *spoke*, and not just with the words that the prophets *wrote*. The revelational experience of the prophets was not limited to canonical writings. All that came through them in the way of 'prophecy' was the very Word of God, whether spoken or written.

These holy men of God spoke as they were 'carried [or borne] along' by the Holy Spirit. B.B. Warfield provides the classic explanation of this phrase:

> What this language of Peter emphasises ... is the passivity of the prophets with respect to the revelation given through them. This is the significance of the phrase: 'It was as borne by the Holy Spirit that men spoke from God.' To be 'borne'... is not the same as to be led ... much less to be guided or directed ... He that is 'borne' contributes nothing to the movement induced, but is the object to be moved. [2]

They were 'borne along' by the Holy Spirit as a ship is carried by the wind. Peter emphasises that there is no exception to this phenomenon as it relates to prophecy. All prophecy is of this sort. Holy men of God spoke as they were 'borne along' by the Holy Spirit.

Peter's representation of the prophetic experience finds full support in the description of Paul. In Ephesians 3:2-3, Paul states: 'Surely you have heard about the administration of God's grace that was given to me for you, that is, the mystery made known to me by revelation.' The New Testament consistently represents a 'mystery' as a truth about God's redemptive programme once concealed, *but now revealed*. This 'mystery' now has been 'revealed' by the Spirit to God's holy apostles and prophets (*Eph.* 3:5). The two offices of apostle and prophet are joined together as the vehicles of divine revelation. Those extraordinary offices were the instruments by which God made known his revelation in the new covenant context. The substance of this 'mystery', once concealed but now revealed, is that the Gentiles are fellow-heirs, fellow-participants, fellow-members in the body of Christ (*Eph.* 3:6).

It is rather interesting that Paul does not speak about a prediction of the future when he refers to the 'mystery' that has been 'revealed'. Instead, he describes insight about a theology of the church. He declares that the 'forth-telling' of the apostles and prophets was revelational. The basic truth they taught about the role of Gentiles in the church was not a prediction about the future, but a divine declaration about the present. Yet it clearly was regarded as 'prophetic' in nature.

Paul's fullest elaboration on the new covenant manifestation of prophecy is found in 1 Corinthians 14. Verses 29 to 33 of this chapter have particular relevance to the subject of the revelatory nature of new covenant prophecy. In the immediately preceding verses Paul declares that the worship services of the church must be ordered to facilitate the proper functioning of the multiplicity of gifts. 'Two or three prophets' may speak while the others are to 'discriminate' (verse 29). The 'others' apparently refer to other prophets. But what is this 'discriminating' which is to occur in connection with the exercise of their gift by the prophets?

The New International Version expands on the word 'discriminate' (which it translates 'weigh carefully') by adding the phrase 'what is said'. The assumption of the translators is that the 'discrimination' to be rendered by the prophets has to do with the *words* that have been spoken. But this assumption overlooks the regular usage in the New Testament of the word 'discriminate'.

The Greek term *diakrino* has the basic meaning of 'to separate, to sever, to make a distinction'. Most frequently it is used to make a distinction among *people*. If we keep before our mind this regular use of the term for 'discriminate', a more precise understanding of the use of the term as it is found in 1 Corinthians 14:29 may be arrived at. 'Two or three prophets should speak, and the other (prophets) should discriminate.' A judgment clearly must be made. But the judgment is not about the words being spoken by the prophets. Instead, a discrimination must be made among persons. Someone must determine who among the prophets is to speak and who is not to speak. This responsibility is entrusted to the prophets, who shall maintain order among their number. Even the utterance of inspired words must be exercised in a framework of order.

Paul assures his readers that all prophets ultimately will have opportunity to speak (verse 31). But he also reminds them that everything must be done decently and in order. For even the spirit of prophets is subject to the prophets (verses 32, 33, 40). So the discrimination in this passage refers to a distinction for the sake of order among prophets, not about the words of the prophets. Some may have to wait until a 'second service'. But all eventually will have the opportunity to deliver the revelation God has granted them.

Equally critical in understanding this passage is the word 'revelation'. A 'revelation' comes first to one, and then a further 'revelation' comes to another (verse 30). This reference to 'revelation' is bracketed by verses concerned with the experience of 'prophecy' (verses 29, 31). Some recent authors suppose that this 'revelation' actually is not a revelation at all. Instead, they think it is something less than a 'prophecy' that is 'revelational' as the term is understood elsewhere in Scripture. The suggestion is that this phenomenon might then be designated a 'non-revelational revelation'. It is revelation from God, it is a prophetic utterance, but somehow it is less than the classic phenomenon of prophecy.

But such an analysis of the intent of Scripture takes a person far from the words of Scripture. The whole context suggests the 'normal' prophetic experience of receiving and delivering an inspired word from the Lord. The first letter to the Corinthians was composed at a time when very little of the New Testament had been written. The church at that stage needed an authoritative word from the Lord to direct the pattern of their life under the new covenant. Very likely none of the inspired manuscripts of the New Testament were available to the Corinthians at this point in time.

Almost certainly the reference in Corinthians was not to an 'illumination' of new covenant Scriptures or new covenant truth already known to them. Instead, the Corinthian church received authoritative, infallible and inerrant 'revelations' of the truths of the new covenant era through the manifold exercise of the gift of prophecy. The prophetic experience that had brought God's word to the old covenant community now communicated the truth about this new era to God's new covenant people. Because God was now manifesting the wonder of the realities of the new covenant, it is not surprising that a manifold display of the prophetic gift occurred in Corinth.

I shall argue in later chapters that the introduction of the concept of a 'non-revelational revelation' could be extremely dangerous when applied to prophetic utterances. For if one prophetic utterance can be designated a 'non-revelational revelation', then any word of prophecy might eventually be declared a 'non-revelational revelation'. In the end, the revelational character of Scripture itself might be redefined in these confusing terms.

A great danger also lies in another direction if we accept this concept of a prophetic utterance that is indeed God's word, and yet is something less than the perfection of his word associated with biblical prophecy. A person is made subject in one sense to a word that supposedly is immediately inspired of God, and yet at the same time by its own definition participates in human fallibility. Even though he knows this supposedly 'prophetic' utterance to be fallible, is the believer none the less to submit as though it came directly from God? Or is he to *resist* yielding to this word that has come immediately from God because he knows it to be fallible?

I am anticipating what will be argued more fully below when I say that this concept of prophecy, as it is being proposed in the church today, creates an intolerable situation, a dilemma of confusion that destroys the meaning of unquestioning obedience to God's word. It is not true to the teaching of the word of God, and has the potential for undermining the basic foundation of a life of trusting obedience to the revelation of God's prophets. It destroys the necessary distinction between the true and the false prophet, and makes God's people the helpless victims of error mixed with truth.

5.   CONCLUSION

The history of prophetism extends backwards to the time of Moses. From his day, God consistently revealed himself to his people through the stream of prophets he had promised Moses. The surety of the prophetic word enabled God's people to resist the pretences of the steady stream of false prophets throughout Israel's history. Joel, recalling the older Mosaic experiences of the prophets, predicted that the new covenant community would enjoy the same kind of prophetic revelation. The apostles Peter and Paul in their turn applied these same descriptions to the prophetic word of their own day. In view of the biblical testimony concerning the nature of prophecy, several conclusions may be proposed.

Firstly, the starting-point of any discussion about prophecy today should begin with the long history of the revelational character of this gift of the Spirit. Throughout the old and new covenant eras, God remains as the originator of the truly prophetic word.

Secondly, the warning of Scripture concerning the dangers of false prophecy must be remembered. If revelation has been completed with the perfection of the New Testament Scriptures, then prophecy as the principal revelational gift has now ceased. The modern preacher may be 'prophetic' in his ministry just as he may be 'apostolic'. But he must beware of claiming for himself either the revelational experience of the prophet or the foundational position of the apostle. Many are the cases both ancient and modern of lives seriously damaged by an improper claim to prophetic utterance.

Thirdly, the biblical testimony concerning prophecy has a critical effect on the question of the role of women in the church. The primary text supporting the speaking of women in worship refers to their 'prophesying' (*1 Cor.* 11:5). If 'to prophesy' means to speak revelationally, then the role of women in the church today is clarified. Only so long as the revelational gift of prophecy remained alive in the church could women serve as instruments of the divine word. But if the prophetic word of God has found its perfection with the completion of the new covenant Scriptures, then the role of women as instruments of divine revelation has now ceased.

The questions raised by the subject of prophecy are not small in significance. They are critical to the health, the well-being and the proper ordering of the church of Jesus Christ today. Let the church be careful that all things are done decently and in order, in accordance with the teachings of the prophetic Scriptures.

Chapter Two

Tongues Today?

The question of 'tongues' in the church today continues to be a source of great difference of opinion. Some people are most enthusiastic. Others are quite certain that the current phenomenon represents Satan's work in the midst of the church. Most evangelical believers simply don't know what to think or how to respond.

How do you decide among these various opinions? You cannot deny that something called 'tongues-speaking' is occurring in the church today. But how do you reach a sound conclusion about its significance?

By the study of Scripture, of course. Certainly it is important to be sensitive to the religious experiences of various people. But ultimately all religious experience must stand the objective test of Scripture. The greatest favour that may be shown to Christian friends is to call them to test their experience by Scripture. For 'iron sharpens iron; so a man sharpens the countenance of his friend' (*Prov.* 27:17).

The possibility of a 'fresh look' at the subject of tongues in Scripture may be viewed with scepticism in the light of the flood of material already available on the subject. But the effort must be made for exegetical re-evaluation.

In the New Testament only two books mention the

phenomenon of tongues, excluding the longer ending of Mark. But in the Old Testament three different authors anticipate the New Testament phenomenon of tongues. Taken together, four different aspects of tongues surface from these old and new covenant Scriptures which point to the same conclusion: the tongues now being manifested in the church are something other than the tongues anticipated in the Old Testament prophecy and realised in the New Testament experience. These four elements are as follows:

1. New Testament tongues were revelational;
2. New Testament tongues were foreign languages;
3. New Testament tongues were for public consumption;
4. New Testament tongues were a sign indicating a radical change in the direction of redemptive history.

Let us consider each of these aspects of biblical tongues as they may contribute to an understanding of the modern phenomenon.

1. NEW TESTAMENT TONGUES WERE REVELATIONAL

If exegetical considerations lead to the conclusion that New Testament tongues were revelational, it follows that unless a person is willing to allow for continuing revelation beyond the Scriptures, the tongues being manifested today cannot be regarded as the same as the tongues of the New Testament. Several considerations point to this conclusion, the first of these being the usage of the term 'mystery' in 1 Corinthians 14 and the rest of the New Testament.

In 1 Corinthians 14:2 Paul says, 'He who speaks in a tongue utters mysteries.' This term '*mysterion*' in the New Testament has a very specific meaning which inherently includes the idea of the communication of divine revelation.

23

As already noted, a 'mystery' in the New Testament is a truth about God's way of redemption that once was concealed *but now has been revealed*. In its very essence a New Testament 'mystery' is a revelational phenomenon. This conclusion is supported by virtually every usage of the term 'mystery' in the New Testament.

The term 'mystery' occurs approximately 28 times in the New Testament. The consistency of meaning maintained in Scripture is striking:

Matthew 13:11: Jesus says, 'To you it is given *to know* the mysteries of the kingdom.' These 'mysteries' are no longer hidden from Jesus' disciples. Kingdom mysteries are truths *revealed* rather than concealed.

Romans 11:25: Paul explains, 'I do not want you to be ignorant of this mystery.' The 'mystery' about Israel should no longer be a matter of ignorance, for the truth of the 'mystery' has been revealed.

Romans 16:25: Paul's preaching is 'according to the *revelation of the mystery* hidden for long ages past *but now revealed and made known*.' Paul can preach with confidence because the 'mystery' of the gospel now has been revealed.

As he begins his letter to the Corinthians, Paul explains: 'I proclaimed to you the mystery of God' (*1 Cor.* 2:1). It was not an enigma that he proclaimed. He declared openly something that needed to be understood. Paul continues in the same vein by noting that Christian ministers speak God's wisdom-in-mystery which *has been* hidden, but now can be openly proclaimed (*1 Cor.* 2:7). So men ought to regard Christian ministers as *stewards* of the mysteries of God (*1 Cor.* 4:7). Since they are stewards dispensing the mysteries, the 'mysteries' are now understood.

1 Corinthians 13:2: Paul proposes the hypothetical case in which he might come to '*know* all mysteries', and in 1 Corinthians 15:51 he declares, 'Behold I *tell* you a mystery.' Throughout his letter to the Corinthians, a 'mystery'

appears as an element of God's redemptive truth that now has become known.

This understanding of 'mystery' continues throughout Paul's writings. In Ephesians 1:9, 'God *made known* the mystery of his will.' It was 'by revelation' that the 'mystery' was made known to Paul (*Eph.* 3:3). He wants the Ephesians to '*know*' his understanding of the 'mystery of Christ' (*Eph.* 3:4). He intends to make plain to everybody what is the 'administration of the mystery which has been kept hidden through all ages' (*Eph.* 3:9). Marriage in Christ is a 'great mystery', but now he is making it known to them. The Ephesians must pray that he will 'fearlessly *make known* the mystery of the gospel' (*Eph.* 6:19,20).

Throughout Colossians, the same significance prevails for the term. In Colossians 1:25 Paul declares: 'I present to you the Word of God in fullness, the mystery kept hidden for ages and generations *but now revealed* to the saints.' He can make known the gospel only because God has 'chosen to *make known* the glorious riches of this mystery' (*Col.* 1:27). Paul has striven that they may *know* the mystery of God (*Col.* 2:2). To this end he asks them to 'pray that we may *proclaim* the mystery of Christ' (*Col.* 4:3)

2 Thessalonians 2:7 is something of an exception to this pattern. It refers to the 'mystery' of lawlessness that has not yet been solved. But in 1 Timothy 3:9 Paul explains that deacons 'must *possess* the mystery of the faith with a clear conscience'. In 1 Timothy 3:16 Paul acknowledges that the 'mystery' of godliness is great. But then he proceeds to explain this mystery as consisting in the truth now made known that 'God was *manifest* in the flesh, justified in the Spirit, *seen* of angels, *preached* to the nations, *believed* on in the world, received up into glory'. His point is that the mystery once hidden has now been made known.

Finally, in the book of Revelation the 'mystery of the seven stars' is explained. The seven stars are the seven churches (*Rev.* 1:20). John subsequently reveals that 'the mystery of God' will be accomplished '*just as he announced to his prophets*' (*Rev.* 10:7). In similar fashion, Babylon is the 'mystery' that the interpreting angel will 'explain' (*Rev.* 17:5-7).

Twenty-eight times the term 'mystery' is used in the New Testament. If we set aside for a moment the occurrence in 1 Corinthians 14 presently under consideration, twenty-seven cases explicitly talk about a 'mystery' as something once hidden *but now revealed*. Christianity emphatically is not a mystery religion. Christianity stands in drastic contrast with numerous other religions built on codes of secrecy. Christianity desires everything to be open and above board. The God of Christianity has nothing to hide. He openly manifests his truth to the world in the same way in which he sends light to dispel the darkness.

In this broader context, the reference to a 'mystery' in 1 Corinthians 14:2 may be properly understood. 'He who speaks in a tongue . . . *utters mysteries*,' says Paul. He does not conceal truth by speaking a 'mystery'. Instead he communicates the truth that has been made known to him by divine revelation. Tongues were a divine instrument for communicating revelation. They were a means by which God disclosed redemptive truth once hidden but now revealed. This interpretation of the term 'mystery' in 1 Corinthians 14:2 would seem to be contradicted at first sight by the remainder of the verse. For Paul says, 'Anyone who speaks in a tongue does not speak to men but to God; indeed *no one understands him*, for he speaks mysteries' (*1 Cor.* 14:2). How could it make good sense that a message spoken in tongues is revelational if it is not understood?

It could make good sense if the 'tongues' described throughout Scripture are foreign languages. If 'tongues' are 'languages' foreign to the speaker which might not be known to the audience, then it would make perfectly good sense that 'he who speaks in a tongue does not speak to men but to God, since no one understands him' (*1 Cor.* 14:2). He speaks as an instrument of revelation, but the language of his revelation is not understood apart from translation. In this regard, the situation at Corinth may be contrasted with the unique circumstance in Jerusalem on the first day of tongues-speaking. On the day of Pentecost, all the various languages of the world were represented by hearers as well as by speakers. So they all heard in their own native tongue the wondrous works of God. But in Corinth it is not likely that all the languages would be represented. As a result, no one would understand the speaker even though he declared the truth of God that was coming to him by revelation. A 'mystery' was being revealed in the utterance of the tongues-speaker, but since no one was familiar with the language he spoke, his revelation was not understood.

In any case, the use of the term 'mystery' as it relates to 'tongues' clearly indicates that tongues were revelational in nature. By the gift of tongues a 'mystery' concerning God's way of redemption was 'revealed' to the new covenant people of God. The revelational character of tongues is further confirmed by Paul's additional words of explanation:

> He who speaks in a tongue edifies himself, but he who prophesies edifies the church. I would like every one of you to speak in tongues; but I would rather have you prophesy. He who prophesies is greater than the one who speaks in tongues, unless he interprets.
>
> (*1 Cor.* 14:4-5, NIV)

According to the last phrase in the above quotation, tongues interpreted are equivalent to prophecy. The message brought in a tongue is brought up to the level of divinely inspired prophecy, once the tongue has been interpreted. If prophecy is a revelational gift (as biblical evidence of both the Old Testament and the New Testament would appear to support), and tongues interpreted are equivalent to prophecy, then tongues also should be understood as a revelational gift.

To understand more fully Paul's point about the relation of tongues and prophecy in the life of the church, the question must be asked: how do words edify? Exactly what was it in the verbal gift of prophecy that 'edified'? Was it the sensations created by the voice of the prophet that edified? Was it the physical vibrations set up in the ears of the hearers that edified? Or was it the emotion experienced by the prophet himself that somehow had the effect of edifying his hearers?

No, it was not the aural sensations in themselves that built up the believers in their most holy faith. It was *the understanding* of God's truth brought about by a revelation through prophecy that edified. By the communication of truth which could be understood and believed the hearers were built up in their faith.

In a similar manner, tongues that were interpreted so that people could understand the revelation became equivalent to prophecy as an instrument of edification. Without interpretation, the observing of someone speaking in a tongue had no edifying effect on the spectator. But once the message spoken in the tongue was interpreted to the audience, edification could occur among them as it had occurred to the speaker. For tongues interpreted were equivalent to prophecy in their ability to edify. Once interpreted, the message spoken in a 'tongue' became the very voice of God to the people.

But a further question must be asked. How is it that tongues had the effect of edifying the *speaker*? Paul plainly states, 'He who speaks in a tongue edifies himself'(*1 Cor.* 14:4). But what in the act of speaking in a tongue caused it to edify? Was it the physical vibration associated with the phenomenon of tongues-speaking that edified the speaker?

Was it the emotion accompanying the experience? Tongues, like prophecy, are a verbal gift; and verbal gifts edify by communicating understanding. Edification through the exercise of a verbal gift does not occur by the physical vibration of the oral chambers. It does not occur through the non-rational stirrings of the emotions. Edification through a verbal gift occurs instead by the speaker's coming to understand and believe the truth that he speaks. Otherwise there is no edification.

Anyone who teaches or preaches the Word of God understands this rudimentary principle about spiritual edification. The preacher knows full well that he is not edified by the mere exercise of his gift for preaching. He must understand and believe what he says if edification for himself is to occur.

If this were not the case, a totally different concept of the way edification occurs would have to be envisaged. For if the Spirit can use merely the exercise of a verbal gift for the speaker's edification apart from his understanding what he says, then the same effect could be experienced by the hearers as well as by the speaker. If the one who spoke in a tongue could be edified even while not understanding what he was saying, could not the congregation expect to be edified in the same way? If the sensations associated with uttering a sound like 'quesrylespoyou' have the capacity for edifying the speaker, why could not those same sensations vibrating in the ears of the hearer have the effect of edifying?

But an audience is not edified one whit, no matter how zealous the speaker may be, if the message is unintelligible. Paul makes this very point. No one is edified when no one understands (*1 Cor.* 14:2). Edification through a verbal gift is linked intrinsically to understanding the utterance.

In accordance with this principle, it must be concluded that tongues edified as they communicated the truth of

29

God first to the speaker and then to the hearer. Apart from understanding, there was no edification. It was the revelational experience of the truth of God directly to the tongues-speaker that caused him to be edified. The experience of the tongues-speaker was a revelational experience in which God brought to him knowledge that had the effect of edifying him.

At this point it is essential to look closely at 1 Corinthians 14:14. For Paul appears to contradict this principle when he says: 'For if I pray in a tongue my spirit prays, but my mind is unfruitful.' This statement may seem to indicate that the one who prays in a tongue fails to understand what he is saying. It might appear that Paul is asserting that his non-rational 'spirit' expresses itself quite effectively as he speaks to God in a tongue. But his 'mind' is 'unfruitful', which seems to indicate that he fails to understand the words he himself has uttered in the tongue.

However, this on-the-surface understanding of the phrase rests on a false dichotomy between the human 'spirit' and the 'mind' as these concepts appear in the New Testament Scriptures. The human 'spirit' (*pneuma*) and the 'mind' (*nous*) cannot be separated so radically from one another. An example of the closeness of their interworking may be illustrated from an incident in the life of Christ. Some of his opponents began to 'think within themselves' that he was blaspheming (*Mark* 2:6). But Jesus 'knew in his spirit' what they were thinking. The word for 'knew' derives from the root for 'mind' (*nous*) as it is found in 1 Corinthians 14:14, while the word for 'spirit' (*pneuma*) is the second word found in the same verse in 1 Corinthians. According to the Gospel, Jesus possessed 'rational knowledge' in his 'spirit', which clearly indicates that the 'spirit' does not contain simply the emotional side of man. 'Mind' and 'spirit' in man communicate with one another. It is a false dichotomy contrary to the scriptural teaching about man that suggests that man's 'spirit' (*pneuma*) is an irrational, purely emotional aspect of man, while his 'mind' (*nous*) refers to his reasoning capacities.

When Paul says, 'My spirit prays' (*1 Cor.* 14:14), he means that from within his soul he offers prayers to God. But this praying 'in his spirit' is not without full rational understanding. As a consequence of this understanding as he prays, he is edified. But at the same time, his 'mind', that instrument by which he would formulate his thoughts for the purpose of communicating them to others, remains 'unfruitful'. It bears no fruit. No one else in the assembly is edified with him, because no one else understands what he has spoken in the tongue. He is edified well enough. But no others are edified because his thoughts are not being communicated to them in a way that they can understand. No one else can join in his prayer because no one else understands the utterance of his 'tongue'. But if the inspired utterance of his spirit is translated into a language known by the people, then they too can be edified along with the speaker.

This understanding of verse 14 finds strong confirmation in the immediately following verses. Paul says to the possessor of the gift of tongues:

> If you are praising God with your spirit, how can one who finds himself among those who do not understand say 'Amen' to your thanksgiving since he does not know what you are saying? You may be giving thanks well enough, but the other man is not edified.
>
> (*1 Cor.* 14:16-17, NIV)

If it is to be presumed that a *speaker* can give thanks 'well enough' without even understanding what he is saying, could not the *hearer* just as well join in to give thanks in his heart without ever understanding what the speaker might be saying?

It would be far more consistent with the true mode of

31

edification through a verbal gift to conclude that the one speaking in the tongue understood what he was saying since he gave thanks adequately. But the hearer could not join him because he did not understand.

It has been supposed that Paul intends to describe a verbal gift which edifies the speaker despite his lack of understanding, but which cannot also edify the hearer. But the evidence points in another direction. The speaker gives thanks well enough because he understands his divinely inspired utterance, even though it comes to him in a language he has never studied. But the utterance 'bears no fruit' of sanctification among the audience because it is not understood by them.

This perspective on verse 14 may be supported by a further consideration of verse 5. Paul says, 'He who prophesies is greater than the one who speaks in a tongue, *unless he interprets*' (*1 Cor.* 14:5). The point is strongly made. Interpreted tongues are equivalent to prophecy. But what was God's intent in prophecy? Why did he institute this form of communication?

God's intent in prophecy was to communicate his verbally-inspired, infallible and inerrant Word to his people. God would not settle for less, because he wanted his people to have a secure deposit of truth. In the same way, God's original intent in inspiring a person to speak his word in a 'tongue' was to give expression to his verbally-inspired infallible and inerrant Word. Tongues interpreted could be equivalent to inspired prophecy only because tongues themselves were a revelational gift. By speaking in tongues a person was delivering the very Word of God, infallible and inerrant in all its parts.

This original intent for tongues could be maintained only if the gift of interpretation also functioned as a gift equivalent in its inspiration to the gifts of tongues and prophecy. Only a translation made under the direct inspiration of the

Holy Spirit could retain the verbally inspired, infallible and inerrant character of the Word of God. Anyone who has attempted a translation of the Bible from Greek to English would understand the necessity of an inspired gift if the preciseness and authority of the original Word from God was to be maintained absolutely perfectly. It is clear from 1 Corinthians 14:28 that the tongues-speaker did not necessarily have the gift of interpretation — a gift that required an exactness which went beyond the understanding of the sense of the revelation possessed by the tongues-speaker.

No claim could be made by any translator of Scripture that his product was identical with the verbally-inspired, infallible and inerrant Word of God as originally given unless he could affirm unequivocally that God himself had been directly and infallibly inspiring the change from one language to another. In any case, Paul indicates in these verses that tongues interpreted are equivalent to prophecy. If prophecy is revelational and tongues interpreted are equivalent to prophecy, then tongues also must be a form of revelation that God used for his church.

For this reason, the tongues being experienced today cannot be regarded as the same as New Testament tongues, apart from opening the door to continuing revelation beyond the Scriptures. The effect of this conclusion would be quite far-reaching, and would include bringing into question the completeness of God's revelation through the apostles and prophets appointed by him to provide a foundation for the church that would remain undisturbed throughout the present age.

2.   TONGUES WERE FOREIGN LANGUAGES

Acts 2:6 makes the point very clearly: 'Each one heard them speaking in his own language.' The testimony throughout the rest of the book of Acts gives no indicator that a different kind of tongue was manifested in the experiences of the church after Pentecost. On the contrary, the evidence supports a continuation of the same kind of 'tongues-speaking' as occurred on the day of Pentecost. In Acts 10, Peter justifies the baptism of the Gentiles who had spoken in tongues, for 'the Spirit came on them *just as it did on us*' (*Acts* 10:47). In reporting his action to the church at Jerusalem, Peter calls special attention to the same point: 'The Holy Spirit came on them *just as it did on us at the beginning*' (*Acts* 11:15). The experience of the Holy Spirit at Caesarea corresponded to the Spirit's baptism that came on the apostles on the day of Pentecost. If the gift of speaking in tongues in Acts 2 involved speaking in a foreign language never studied, then the same explanation would apply to the experience of tongues as manifested among the Gentiles in Caesarea. In this light, it may be assumed that the same explanation would apply to the gift of tongues manifested in Ephesus (*Acts* 19:7). It may be worth noting that the experience of tongues in Ephesus occurred after Paul's visit to Corinth (cf. *Acts* 18:1-19). While no specific description characterises the tongues-speaking in Ephesus, the use of the identical language used to describe the phenomenon in Ephesus as had been used in previous narratives in Acts strongly suggests that the nature of the 'tongues' in Ephesus corresponded to the 'tongues' mentioned by Luke throughout the book of Acts.

No mention is made of a tongues-speaking occurrence at Corinth in the book of Acts (cf. *Acts* 18:1-18). But according to Paul's first letter to the Corinthians, the phenomenon of tongues obviously had a prominent role in their church life.

What was the nature of this phenomenon at Corinth? It would seem rather strange indeed if before and after Corinth as described in Acts one kind of 'tongue' manifested itself while at Corinth a totally different phenomenon appeared — and that without any elaboration in Acts of a supposed difference. In both Acts and 1 Corinthians the same terminology is used. Acts 2:4 speaks of 'other tongues', and 1 Corinthians 14:21 similarly refers to 'other tongues'. The Greek is almost identical in both places, and may be translated 'other languages' in each case. Furthermore, 1 Corinthians 14 employs an Old Testament quotation clearly speaking about foreign languages to explain the phenomenon in Corinth (*1 Cor.* 14:21, cf. *Isa.* 28:11,12, *Deut.* 28:49). As a result, it may be concluded that either Paul is making an application of an Old Testament passage that does not strictly apply, or that the tongues of 1 Corinthians 14 were foreign languages as anticipated in the Old Testament passage cited by Paul. Still further, the tongues of 1 Corinthians 14 were translatable, which would suggest that they were foreign languages. Even if it were concluded that these 'languages' of 1 Corinthians were the 'tongues of angels', they still were languages that were translatable into human equivalents.

Strong cumulative evidence supports the conclusion that the tongues of the New Testament times, both in Acts and in 1 Corinthians, were foreign languages. The effect of this conclusion is to place a large portion of modern tongues-speaking activity outside the realm of valid New Testament experience from the outset. Whatever may be going on today, it is not the kind of worship-experience described by the Scriptures of the New Testament.

In this regard, one view that has been promoted widely in recent days must be rejected, not for its initial points but for its rather unexpected conclusion. This particular viewpoint begins by affirming that the tongues described in the New Testament were for public usage in the church. It is furthermore asserted that the tongues of today must be regarded as something other than the phenomenon of tongues described in the New Testament Scriptures.

But in the end it is proposed that the tongues of today, though not of the nature of New Testament tongues, are nonetheless a gift of the Spirit to the modern church. Though admittedly not the same as the tongues of the New Testament, it is said that they have a proper role in the life of God's people today. Because of the frantic pace of modern life, God's Spirit has devised this means by which the modern-day, stressed-out Christian may find emotional and psychological relief. Through 'speaking in tongues', an answer may be found to the tensions associated with living in today's world.

Obviously this conclusion cannot arise from an exegesis of Scripture, since the position affirms that the tongues of the New Testament are not the same as modern-day 'tongues'. Instead, it is being proposed that the public assemblies of God's people be opened to a most spectacular phenomenon on the basis of psychological observations concerning the possible effects of tongues-speaking. Modern-day tongues are presented as a legitimate element in worship today on the basis of a hypothesis about the way God might decide to meet the special emotional stresses of the modern world.

But is it to be supposed that the apostle Paul had no need for emotional relief from the tensions associated with his 'care of all the churches' (2 Cor. 11:28)? Should it be concluded that Martin Luther had no need of the 'psychological relief' that comes from the supposedly modern gift of tongues? With kings and governors constantly seeking his life, did Luther have a less stressful situation than Christians in the world today?

Many activities can function as psychological reliefs. Going out to eat, watching a video, or playing a game of golf can serve to uplift the spirit. Yet none of these things should be viewed as a 'gift' of the Spirit. Spiritual gifts are special administrations of the Holy Spirit by which members of Christ's body nourish and minister to one another. To suggest that the modern tongues phenomenon is not of the same nature as the tongues of the New Testament and yet is a gift of the Spirit for the church today could open the door to almost any kind of experience-centred phenomenon.

It would appear much more consistent with the biblical evidence to acknowledge that because the tongues of the first century were foreign languages, the tongues of today, which do not appear to be foreign languages, must be regarded as a phenomenon not endorsed by the New Testament Scriptures.

3. NEW TESTAMENT TONGUES WERE FOR PUBLIC CONSUMPTION, NOT PRIVATE USE

All gifts of the Spirit were for the benefit of Christ's church. A 'gift' in the New Testament was bestowed on an individual so that he might provide a blessing for the people of God. By a 'gift' of the Spirit, one person is enabled to minister to others. Rudimentary to the whole concept of gifts is the fact that they are not for private consumption, but are given for the sake of edifying the body of Christ. Paul says:

> There are different kinds of gifts, but the same Spirit. There are different kinds of service, but the same Lord. There are different kinds of working, but the same God works all of them in all men. Now to each one the manifestation of the Spirit is given for the common good. (*1 Cor.* 12:4-7, NIV)

It is with this understanding in mind that Paul proceeds to develop the image of the church as a body. Each part of the body is given a ministry by which it may aid the rest of the body. The eye keeps the body from stumbling. The mouth feeds the body its nourishment. The ear hears for the rest of the body. All the various gifts enable the members of Christ's body to minister to one another.

With this larger picture of the public nature of spiritual gifts in mind, consider more closely 1 Corinthians 14:18-19. Paul says:

> I thank God that I speak in tongues more than all of you. But in the church I would rather speak five intelligible words to instruct others than ten thousand words in a tongue.

Now, at first glance it seems that Paul intends to contrast private tongues with public tongues. Is not Paul saying, 'I thank God that [*privately*] I speak in tongues more than all of you, but [*publicly*] in the church I would rather speak intelligible words that instruct others?' The contrast between private words spoken in a tongue and public words spoken in prophecy seems to be underscored by his usage of the phrase 'in the *church*' only in conjunction with the 'intelligible words' of prophecy.

But the interpreter must be very careful about introducing words or concepts that do not appear in the original text of Scripture. As a matter of fact, the word order of verse 18 in the original language makes quite plain the true contrast intended by Paul in these verses. It is not a contrast between private and public utterances. Instead, Paul is contrasting his experience in speaking in tongues, in the advancement of Christ's kingdom in general, with the practice of those who were so eager to promote tongues in the church at Corinth. 'More than all of you,' he says, 'I speak in tongues.' Paul's emphasis is made plain by the order of his words. 'In relation to *all of you*, I speak more in tongues' (verse 18). The comparison is between Paul and those of the Corinthian church who are so interested in promoting tongues-speaking. Perhaps to their surprise, Paul affirms that he speaks in tongues more than the whole lot of them.

Then in the next verse he introduces his contrast. 'But with reference to *the church* I prefer to speak five words for understanding' (verse 19). This, then, is Paul's contrast. It is not a contrast between private tongues and prophecy spoken in the church. Instead, the contrast is between tongues as they relate to those who are promoting tongues among the Corinthians and tongues as they relate to the church as a whole. Paul says, 'In relating to you, my record is plain. Recognise this fact. Don't talk to me about speaking in tongues as though I know nothing about the matter, for I have spoken in tongues more than all of you. I know first-hand about speaking in tongues. *But* with reference to the *church*, I would prefer to speak clearly in a language that will edify. Although I do as a matter of fact speak in tongues more than all of you, my concern is for edification.'

That is the contrast in verses 18 and 19. No mention is made of private tongues in contrast with public tongues. For New Testament tongues were never meant for private consumption. Like all other gifts of the Spirit, they were intended for the whole body. With this perspective in view, it becomes clear at the outset that a vast majority of tongues-speaking activity today could not be the same as New Testament tongues. Private tongues are not New Testament tongues. If tongues are a gift for the church, they should be brought out into the open for the benefit of the church.

Endorsement of the idea of a 'private' gift of tongues may lead to a peculiar situation. Suppose a man affirms his sense of call to the ministry. The church responds by indicating its desire to test his gifts. He affirms that in his judgment he has the gift of preaching, so the church tests that gift. He says that he senses in himself the gift of administration. So the church tests that gift.

But what if this candidate for the gospel ministry declares that he also has the gift of tongues? Shall the church also test that gift? Or shall it be concluded that tongues are a 'private' gift that cannot be tested? Strange indeed would be such a circumstance. A person concludes that he possesses a gift meant for the body, and yet his gift cannot be tested. Every other gift of the Spirit must be tested publicly by the church. But a category of gifts is being introduced that cannot be subjected to the testing of the brothers. This kind of circumstance in the church would be strange indeed.

Yet one other verse must be analysed carefully with respect to the possibility of 'private' gifts in the church. For 1 Corinthians 14:28 states that if no 'interpreter' is present to provide the meaning of an utterance spoken in a tongue, then the speaker must keep silent in the church, and must 'speak to himself and to God'. Does not this statement appear to endorse a private gift which does not function publicly in the church?

If approached in a certain way, this verse admittedly would appear to endorse the privatisation of the gift of tongues-speaking. If no interpreter is present, the tongues-speaker should 'speak to himself and to God'.

But further consideration would not appear to lend support to this position. For the whole point of the passage is to provide orderly control of multiple gifts as they function in the church. 'Two or at the most three' should speak in tongues, and someone must interpret (verse 27). In a similar way, 'two or three prophets' should speak, and the others should discriminate (verse 29). The whole context deals with the orderly functioning of gifts within the assembly. In the context of this precise discussion, Paul makes the point that the tongues-speaker without an interpreter is to remain silent, speaking to himself and to God (verse 28). The two actions are simultaneous. As he restrains himself until an interpreter is present, he speaks within himself while communing with God.

The question is not whether the gift of tongues should function in private or in public. Instead, the question is when the gift of tongues may function in the assembly, and the answer is that tongues may function properly in the church only when an interpreter is present. From the comment in verse 31 that 'all can prophesy' in due time, it may be assumed that the same principle would hold for tongues. As soon as an interpreter is present, the utterance may be delivered. But in the meantime, the tongues-speaker must manifest patience in the assembly, just like the prophet. For the spirits of all prophets are subject to the orderly control of prophets.

In any case, the context presumes the public functioning of the gifts. The verbal gifts of tongues and prophecy are intended for the whole community, not merely for an individual to exercise in private. A person may justify the private exercise of 'tongues' from personal experience. He may testify to the fact that he derives great relief from tension through letting his vocalisations in prayer run ahead of his rational processess. His 'prayer-language' is to him a 'gift' from God that helps him cope with life today.

But in the end, experience must be judged by Scripture, and not vice versa. It may be that the groanings of prayer sometimes express such deep emotions that they are not easily framed into rational expressions. But these kinds of experiences should not be identified with the tongues of the New Testament unless a convincing exegetical argument can establish that point.

4.   NEW TESTAMENT TONGUES WERE A SIGN

Tongues served as a signal from God concerning the fulfilment of particular prophecies about a dramatic change in the direction of God's procedure for working in the world.

41

God does not often surprise his people with something totally unexpected. He prepares them so that they can understand what he is doing. This rudimentary principle about the way of God's working in the world applies to the manifestation of the gift of tongues in New Testament times. Prophecy and fulfilment, preparation and realisation work together for the edification and enlightenment of God's people.

An elder in a church outside Chicago, Illinois does stunt-flying for a hobby. Taking a ride with a stunt pilot can be great fun, provided you are properly prepared.

'Want to take a little spin?'

'Sure, let's go up! Just don't surprise me with any un-expected manoeuvres.'

'Okay, let's start with a little loop. But be prepared. You will experience a certain "G" factor — a "gravity" pull. Your skin will feel as though it's about to pull right through the skeletal outline of your face. That's the "gravity" factor.'

Next he announces the 'hammerhead'. In this man-oeuvre, the nose of the aeroplane points straight upward. The plane climbs heavenward until gravity overcomes the pulling power of the engine. When the motor begins to die, the plane falls sideways. You hope the engine will catch again as you plummet downward. That is stunt flying. Once you have been properly prepared for the various manoeuvres, you should have no problem.

In a much more reasonable fashion, God prepares his people for what is coming in the realm of redemption. He does not startle his people with surprises. God did not suddenly introduce the phenomenon of tongues as some-thing wholly new on the day of Pentecost. Old Testament prophecies set the stage for the tongues that were to come.

We have already noted Peter's reference to the prophecy of Joel on the day of Pentecost (*Acts* 2:16-21). When the twelve apostles began to speak in languages they had never studied, Peter indicated that they were fulfilling Joel's prophecy. Joel had prepared God's people for that moment by stating that in the last days God would pour out his Spirit on all flesh. He prophesied that sons and daughters would *speak in tongues*.

Is that what Joel said?

No, that is not what Joel said.

What did Joel say? He said that sons and daughters would *prophesy*. Yet Pentecost is clearly characterised as the great day of tongues-speaking.

Has Peter perverted Scripture? Has he twisted Joel's prophecy to make it say what he wanted to hear?

No, he has not. But his application of Joel's prophecy to 'tongues' points to a basic understanding about the nature of tongues. Tongues must be regarded as a subset of prophecy. So Joel's prediction about prophecy in the last days gave some preparation for the phenomenon of tongues. From Peter's application of Joel's words on the day of Pentecost, it becomes clear that tongues are a form of prophecy.

But even more significant for understanding the basic nature of tongues is the citation from Isaiah by the apostle Paul in 1 Corinthians 14:21. His Old Testament quotation actually refers to 'other tongues'.

'Tongues' are mentioned explicitly in the Old Testament no less than three times. Three different authors in three different books of the Old Testament explicitly prophesy about tongues. In each case the Old Testament Scriptures indicate that tongues are a sign of covenantal curse for Israel.

Paul quotes one of these prophecies about tongues in 1 Corinthians 14:20-22. 'Brothers, stop thinking like children. In regard to evil be infants, but in your thinking be adults' (*1 Cor.* 14:20). The people in Corinth were being childish about their use of the gift of tongues. They were using this gift from God as though it were a toy. They did not care whether or not others understood the meaning of the tongue.

Paul says, 'Stop being childish.' A two-year-old may squeeze food through his fist and eat his meal off his knuckles. But at some point he needs to stop being childish. In the same way, a gift of God may be used in a childish way. Paul urges the Corinthians to stop being childish in their tongues-speaking. He grounds his admonition in an Old Testament scripture that speaks about 'other tongues'. He says,

> In the Law it is written: 'Through men of strange tongues and through the lips of foreigners I will speak to this people, but even then they will not listen to me,' says the Lord. (*1 Cor.* 14:21, NIV)

By this quotation from Isaiah 28, Paul sets tongues-speaking in the context of the history of redemption. He demonstrates an accurate understanding of the context of his quotation. The prophet had asked: 'Who is [God] trying to teach? To whom is he explaining his message?' (*Isa.* 28:9a). Then the prophet answers his own question: 'To children weaned from their milk, to those just taken from the breast' (*Isa.* 28:9b, NIV).

The people of God in Isaiah's day had anticipated the problem of childishness that was so obvious to Paul among the Corinthians in their use of spiritual gifts. The prophet had then depicted vividly the rudimentary way in which instruction had to be communicated from the Lord to his infantile people:

> For it is:
> Line upon line, line upon line,
> rule on rule, rule on rule;
> a little here, a little there. (*Isa.* 28:10)

Because of their childishness, God must speak to his people like children. A rule here, a command there. 'Don't run in the street. Put your napkin in your lap. Go and make your bed.'

Then the prophet had pronounced God's judgment on the people for their folly: 'Very well, then, with foreign lips and with strange tongues I will speak to this people' (*Isa.* 28:11). If you will not hear the plain word of God in your native tongue, then God will speak to you in a foreign language. He will speak to you so that you will hear words just as an infant hears the conversation of the adult world. If you are going to act like a baby, then God will speak to you like a baby.

The baby sits in the middle of the floor with his cookie and milk. He eats his cookie and pours his milk on the floor. Mother returns to the room. She begins to talk to the baby. What does the baby hear? The baby hears what sounds like gobbledy-gook. Because the baby cannot understand the language of an adult, he hears the words of his mother as though they were babblings.

But more particularly, the baby hears words of judgment. Isaiah says that the 'tongues' of foreigners will represent the arrival of God's judgment for Israel. When the unrepentant nation hears men who have invaded their land speaking in foreign languages, they must recognise it as a sign that God has brought his judgment of an alien army on them. The army of the 'babbling Babylonians' represents for Israel a return of the judgment that first brought the confusion of tongues at the tower of 'Babel'.

But eighth-century Isaiah was not the first to speak of foreign languages as a sign of judgment for God's people. As far back as the time of Moses, foreign tongues represented the arrival of God's judgment. One of the most awesome passages in Scripture describes the curses of the covenant that would come to a disobedient Israel. Among these curses that were sure to fall on the covenant-breaker was the following:

45

> The Lord will bring a nation against you from far away,
> from the ends of the earth, like an eagle swooping down,
> a nation whose *tongue you will not understand.*
>
> (*Deut.* 28:49, NIV)

In this prophetic context dating back to the days of Moses, the significance of tongues is clear. Tongues serve as a sign that judgment has come for Israel. The threat of covenantal curses must be fulfilled because Israel will fail to hear the Word of God. This same message recurs once more a hundred and fifty years after Isaiah in the days of Jeremiah. From Moses to Isaiah to Jeremiah the significance of tongues for Old Testament prophecy is the same.

Jeremiah lived in the day of the Babylonian conquest of Palestine. The prophet anticipates the judgment that was to fall in his day:

> 'O House of Israel,' declares the Lord, 'I am bringing a
> distant nation against you – an ancient and enduring na-
> tion, a people whose tongue you do not know, whose
> speech you do not understand.'   (*Jer.* 5:15)

Once more tongues serve as a sign of covenantal judgment on a disobedient nation. When the 'babbling Babylonians' invade Israel, speaking their strange dialect, then God's covenant people will know that judgment has come on them.

So Scripture presents a unified testimony about the significance of tongues. Prophecies from the fifteenth century B.C., from the eighth century B.C., and from the sixth century B.C. all unite to make the same point. When foreign languages overrun Israel, they will be a sign that God's judgment has come.

In the light of this larger Old Testament context of specific prophecies concerning tongues, Paul's explanation of the passage from Isaiah becomes more understandable. 'Tongues,' he says, 'are a sign' (*1 Cor.* 14:22). Tongues are a sign, and a sign is not to be regarded as an end in itself.

A sign points to something else. A sign serves as an indicator, highlighting another object worth noting. A sign may indicate a change in the direction of the road ahead. It may indicate a curve in the road which will force a turn toward a different direction. In this case, tongues function as a sign in the history of redemption indicating that God is making a change.

What is the change that God was making when he introduced tongues at the beginning of the new covenant era? God was indicating that he no longer would speak a single language to a single people. At least since the time of Moses, he had spoken one language to one people. But now, by the gift of tongues at Pentecost, God indicates that he intends to speak in many languages to many peoples. He will speak in all the languages of the world to all peoples of the world.

Tongues, therefore, mark a point of drastic change in the direction of God's work in the world. On the one hand, tongues signified a distinctive judgment for Israel. Jesus speaks of this same judgment when he says, 'The kingdom shall be taken from you and given to a people bringing forth the fruit thereof' (*Matt.* 21:43).

When the people of Israel heard the foreign tongues of the Babylonians in the streets of Jerusalem, they were experiencing the fulfilment of the prophecies of old. They had persisted too far and too long in the rejection of the words spoken so clearly by God.

In a similar way, the foreign tongues spoken on the day of Pentecost were a sign of covenantal curse for Israel. No longer would God speak exclusively to them in contrast with all the nations of the world. But at the same time, tongues at Pentecost served as a sign of the great blessing of God to all the nations of the world, including Israel. Tongues were a sign of the extension of the blessing of the covenant to all the nations of the world. For even though

God took the kingdom from the Jews, he also grafted believers from among them back into the kingdom by his mercy and grace.

For this reason, tongues should be seen as a dramatic sign at a very specific point in redemptive history. They marked the transition to a truly world-wide gospel. For this reason, tongues played a significant role in the history of redemption.

But inherent in the nature of a sign is its temporally limited character. A sign marking a curve in the road is no longer needed by the traveller once the change of direction has been made. The traveller does not grasp hold of the sign so that he can take it along with him. Once the turn has been made, the sign has completed its usefulness.

Once the world might have presumed that Christianity was a Jewish religion. Christianity began with a Jewish Messiah and twelve Jewish apostles. But God gave an indicator to the world in the foundational age of the apostles that made it plain that any man from any nation who called on the name of the Lord could participate equally with Israel in the blessings of the messianic kingdom. God spoke in many languages so that everybody could hear. Gentiles as well as Jews had the opportunity to understand in their own tongue that they too were invited to participate in Christ's kingdom.

Tongues illustrated dramatically the universalistic character of Christianity. God was not limiting himself to one people. His wondrous works could be heard in all the languages of the world. Tongues were a dramatic sign of a change of direction. Christianity was not exclusively a 'Jewish' religion, despite its clearly Jewish origins.

Once the need for a sign to indicate the universal characteristic of Christianity was obvious. But who today would be in danger of thinking that Christianity was a 'Jewish' religion? The need for a sign of transition exists no longer.

By the gift of tongues God made it obvious to all that he had moved from speaking one language to the world to speaking all the languages of the world to all the peoples of the world.

Tongues are a sign, a sign that is no longer needed. Indeed, in their day they also served the purpose of being a mode of revelation. For tongues interpreted were equivalent to prophecy. They were the very words of God which, when rightly understood, could edify the church of God. But just as the church no longer needs a sign establishing its world-wide character, so neither does the church need the revelation of new divine truth that tongues might supply. No further prophetic word is needed because the fullness of the word of prophecy has been preserved in Scripture.

The church needs neither pseudo-prophetism nor pseudo-tongues. It needs no diversion from the plain declaration of the divine mystery that now is revealed in all its fullness. The one thing the church and the world needs today is the faithful proclamation of the Word of God once given. It needs no more.

This continuing need for the clear proclamation of the prophetic Word now found in Scripture is brought out by Paul as he continues his explanation of the phenomenon of tongues as predicted in the Old Testament: 'Tongues are a sign, not for believers but for *unbelievers*' (*1 Cor.* 14:22). Tongues clearly indicate God's judgment on unbelief. If the Lord would bring such devastating judgment on his old covenant people as the Babylonians brought on Israel, then he surely will bring a finalising judgment of even greater proportions on all who hear and reject the gracious message of the new covenant. This new covenant judgment was demonstrated to all when by the gift of tongues God turned from speaking one language to one people and dramatically demonstrated his intentions to speak many languages to many peoples.

But the gospel of the new covenant cannot rest with communicating a symbol of God's righteous judgment. It must move on to the clear proclamation of the message of salvation in words calculated to lead men to repentance. So Paul continues. The assembly of Christians must not rest contented with the manifestation of the gift of tongues, the sign of judgment given over the unbeliever. If the unbeliever is to be convinced that he is a sinner, the spokesmen in the assembly must move on from tongues to prophecy (*1 Cor.* 14:24). Then the secrets of his heart will be laid bare, he will fall down to worship God, and will perceive the presence of God among the people (*1 Cor.* 14:25). It is prophecy, not tongues, that ultimately will make believers out of unbelievers (*1 Cor.* 14:22b).

For this reason, prophecy (in its finalised, inscripturated form) will continue its active role in the life of the church throughout the present age. Until Christ returns in glory, the 'more sure word of prophecy' found in Scripture serves the church as the divine instrument for the conviction and conversion of sinners (*2 Pet.* 1:19). It is that living and powerful Word, the two-edged sword that pierces to the dividing asunder of soul and spirit, and is a discerner of the thoughts and intents of the heart (*Heb.* 4:12).

5. CONCLUSION

Tongues, as in the case of all the other workings of God in the world, find their significance when located properly in the history of redemption. The barrier-breaking experience of the apostolic church at Pentecost allowed it to proclaim the gospel in all languages of the world. When seen in its unique historical setting as a sign of transition to a world-wide gospel, tongues give greatest glory to the universal gospel. While tongues served as a sign, the fuller role of inscripturated prophecy now must be allowed its permanent place of continuing priority as the church progresses from age to age, proclaiming the message of the prophetic Scriptures in the power of the Holy Spirit to men of all nations.

Chapter Three

Revelation Today?

'What is the chief end of' ... revelation? Perhaps you did not expect the question to end that way. The familiar form of the query is: 'What is the chief end of ... man?' The change in the classic question from the Shorter Catechism is not intended to create confusion but to encourage a look at the question of the 'end' of revelation from a more positive perspective. For coming to an 'end' can mean arriving at a glorious goal.

Think of the end of revelation for a moment in terms of arriving at its goal. What has been the goal of God's revealing himself to sinful men all through the ages? Has the goal been that man might forever have dreams about God? That he might strain continually to make out the exact shape of a vision of deity? Or that he might puzzle through eternity, trying to put into some coherent whole the many odd-shaped pieces of random information about God that keep coming from heaven?

No. It should be obvious. The end-goal of 'revelation' is not the perpetual experience of revelation itself. Revelation instead is a means to an end. It is the way by which the eternal God makes himself known to sinful men who are hopelessly lost apart from his Son the Lord Jesus Christ.

Revelation has as its end the making known to men of the one and only God, and Jesus Christ whom he has sent.

Viewed from this perspective, the 'end' of revelation is not something to be regretted. As a matter of fact, 'the sooner the better' might be the more natural attitude toward the 'end' of revelation. The sooner a piecemeal process of revelation has been completed, the quicker men can come to know personally and intimately the God who loves sinners in all his fullness as the redeemer of men. So the question may be asked, 'Where are we now in this process of the self-revelation of God to sinners? Where do we stand in relation to the end?'

The writer to the Hebrews answers that question quite specifically. He recalls the diverse circumstances and ways in which God revealed himself in the past. But noting that the last stage of human history finally has arrived, he asserts that God has now spoken definitively by the embodiment of all truth in the person of his Son (*Heb.* 1:1). So far as the present form of man's existence is concerned, the end has come! The goal of revelation has been realized! In Jesus Christ revelation from God, in so far as the present era is concerned, has reached its climax. Through knowing him, sinful man today reaches the limit of his capacity to know personally his creator and redeemer.

It is in this context of the arrival of the 'fullness of time' as planned by God that the matter of the end of revelation must be viewed. The termination of revelational activity by God must not be mourned as though it were something like the decease of a favoured friend. Instead it should be viewed as the full opening of a jewelled chest that exposes to view the priceless treasure within. As decoratively beautiful as the chest may be, the substance of the thing is to be found in the full revelation of the treasure within.

So now the stage is set for considering more positively this question of the 'end' of revelation. Revelation must not be viewed as an end in itself, a phenomenon that should be expected to perpetuate its own existence forever. Revelation has as its goal the personal knowledge of Christ himself, who is the yea and amen of all the promising words of God. So in that context we shall consider exactly what it means that in so far as the present age is concerned, the process of revelation has ceased in view of its reaching its goal with the coming of Christ.

1. WHAT IT MEANS THAT REVELATION HAS CEASED

a. *To say that revelation has ceased because it has come to its end-goal in the person of Jesus Christ does not mean that God has stopped revealing himself in nature and through the works of providence.* The heavens continue to declare the glory of God, and the firmament shows his handiwork (*Ps.* 19:1). God still makes known his power and godhead through the works of creation and providence (*Rom.* 1:18-20). Lessons may be learned about the character of God in his justice and mercy through observing his dealings with men and nations. Whenever tyrants are brought down, the truth of God is vindicated and manifested. But none of this revelation explains the way by which sinful men may be redeemed and restored to fellowship with their creator. It may prepare for Christ, lay a foundation for understanding the need for redemption from sin that condemns. But this ongoing revelation of God's eternal power and godhead does not unveil the identity of the Saviour, the nature of the work by which he delivers men, or the means by which people become participants in his powerful redemption. The 'revelation' of these special truths has its end in Jesus Christ, and can reach its fullness only in him.

b. *The fact that revelation has reached its end or goal in the coming of Jesus Christ does not mean that God has stopped speaking and communicating with men through the Scriptures.* The Spirit of God continues to illumine the truths of the Bible so that the hearts and minds of men can understand and believe. Affirming that special revelations about Jesus no longer occur does not mean that God no longer communes and communicates with his people. By the work of the Spirit in the hearts of men, millions of people all over the world daily come to a better understanding of the truth of God as found in the Bible. Constantly he leads men, women and children into a deeper understanding of the truths of the word of God. It is not even necessary to be in the process of reading the Bible for God's Spirit to communicate his truth in this way. As a person drives along the highway, as he rakes leaves outdoors, does the dishes, speaks to a friend, wrestles in prayer, new insight may be gained into the meaning of the word of God for life. God is alive, and it is with this living God that the Christian communes constantly on the basis of truths revealed in the Bible.

But this kind of regular experience known to every Christian is not the same thing as 'revelation'. To assert that is not to quibble about terms. Paul himself at times may speak of God's 'revealing' new insight into his truth as it applies to life (*Eph.* 1:17, *Phil.* 3:15). But these common experiences fall into an entirely different category than God's special revelation of new truth about Jesus Christ, his work, and the future of the world. You may have insight about the Christian character of a person named Mary that would lead you to conclude that she ought to marry John. But do not make the mistake of concluding that your 'insight' is a 'word from the Lord' that should be declared as God's word to the couple. For nothing in the Bible, which is the only source of God's special revelation today, could lead to that conclusion. You may be a keen economic analyst. But do not think that you can announce as a 'word from the Lord' that Christians should prepare for a depression that certainly must come next year. For God's word as found in the Bible, having reached its climax in Christ, does not convey specific information about tomorrow. It is this special kind of revelation that has ceased, even though the illumination of the revealed word of Scripture as it applies to concrete situations in the lives of individuals occurs constantly.

c. *The end of revelation does not mean merely that no further additions may be made to the collection of inspired writings that make up the canon of Scripture.* Over the centuries the church has recognized that the authoritative writings of the Bible are unique. No more books, chapters, verses or words are to be added to these materials. They stand alone as the authoritative voice of God in the world, declaring his will for man's salvation. The assertion that revelation has ended certainly includes the idea that nothing can be added to the Holy Scriptures.

But even the most ardent Pentecostalist would agree with this principle. Who would presume to claim that written materials which he had composed ought to be incorporated into Scripture? Because this principle is so generally granted, it cannot be the point of concern about the 'end' of revelation. The true matter of concern in current debate becomes apparent when it is recognized that the assertion that 'revelation has ceased' involves more than simply affirming a closed collection of authoritative, inspired writings. It means more comprehensively that no further inspired, authoritative communications come to people other than those that are found in the Bible.

Throughout the ages before the completion of Scripture, revelation concerning the way of man's redemption included more material than that which finally found its way into the collection of writings called the Bible. This point is clearly seen when the teaching activity of Jesus is considered. The end of John's Gospel includes two statements that are relevant to this point. As he concludes his presentation of the Christ, John says:

> Jesus did many other miraculous signs in the presence of his disciples which are not recorded in this book ... Jesus did many other things as well. If every one of them were written down, I suppose that even the whole world would not have room for the books that would be written.   (*John* 20:30; 21:25)

These are words which are almost guaranteed to make us curious. What were the many other 'signs' and 'things' done by Jesus that the Gospels have not recorded? What was the message communicated by these signs? If the healing of the man born blind revealed that Jesus was the light of the world, and the feeding of the five thousand revealed that Jesus was the bread of life, what wondrous things about Jesus did these other signs make known about the Saviour? These kinds of questions, however, are to be met by the fact that we have in the record of the Bible all we need to know about Jesus.

This great truth must be put before those who now hope and expect that perhaps Christ will come to them and perform similar signs that would reveal things about himself today. Some groups, such as the Roman Catholic Church, encourage their adherents to hope for a miraculous sign in our day. With its long tradition of continuing miracles, this Church would see every reason to believe that Christ would keep coming back to make himself known more fully.

But the affirmation that special revelation reached its goal so far as the present age is concerned, and therefore ceased with the coming of Christ into the world, means that this kind of experience should not be expected today. It is not simply that the canon in terms of a collection of inspired writings has been closed. It is not simply that no more books, chapters, verses or words should be added to the Bible. It is that all the different ways by which God infallibly communicated his will to his people have ceased, for all his previous self-revelations were 'canonical' in that they were authoritative, inspired communications from God. The end of revelation means that all revelatory signs and wonders have stopped until the end of this age. We may not know all about Christ that we might like, but we have in Scripture the record of all we need to know for life and godliness (*2 Tim.* 3:16-17).

Another point must be made to reinforce the affirmation that revelation has ceased. Think once more about the words quoted above from the Gospel of John about the 'many other signs' and the 'many other things' that Jesus did. Clearly during his lifetime Jesus spoke many other words as well as those recorded in the Gospels. During his thirty years on earth he said many more things than those set down in the Bible. How much more we would know about him if all he said while on earth had been recorded! Even the incidental remarks he made could disclose much about the person of our Saviour. 'I must be in my Father's house,' he said as a young boy (*Luke* 1:49). What a revelation those words make to us about the self-consciousness of Jesus as the unique Son of the heavenly Father at the age of twelve. We are thankful for the knowledge of him that comes through the recording of this little cameo. Yet he must have said many other things that would tell us more about his person. We furthermore know that every word that Jesus spoke must have been the inspired, infallible word of God. All his words were revelational, whether or not they have been preserved in the Gospels.

But we can trust the superintendence of the Holy Spirit over the Gospel writers. We know that the highly selective reporting that they did was directed by God's Spirit. Nevertheless, the point must be recognized, special revelation about Christ included far more than the record of his words as found in the Bible.

This principle would be true of the utterances of the prophets in Old Testament times as well. They held their sacred offices for decades. Isaiah, Jeremiah and Ezekiel all functioned as prophets for over forty years apiece. Is it to be assumed that the prophetic utterances that they spoke are limited to the words preserved in the Bible? It is not very likely. Of course, it need not be supposed that every word the prophets spoke was an inspired revelational utterance, as was the case with Jesus. But it would seem quite certain that they spoke many revelational words, had many revelational dreams, performed many revelational signs that are not recorded in Scripture.

To assert that all revelation has ceased is to affirm that none of these kinds of experiences occur any more. It is not merely saying that nothing in the way of new revelation can be added to the Bible. Instead, it is affirming that all the various kinds of special revelations found their consummation in Jesus Christ. He was the goal to which they all pointed. All revelation is completed in him. No more materials in the way of 'rules' or 'canons' are to function as the word of God in the church.

The language of an important confessional document of the church makes this point very plainly. The Westminster Confession of Faith states that God was pleased 'to reveal himself' at various times and in a variety of ways. Then he committed the revelation of himself 'wholly [that is, exclusively] unto writing'. It is not that everything that God revealed to men throughout the ages was written down, as the unrecorded signs and sayings of Jesus clearly indicate. Instead, this affirmation of the Westminster Confession means that in terms of the method by which he would make himself known, God has stopped speaking in signs, wonders, visions and prophecies. Now he uses exclusively the form of written-down revelations preserved for all generations in the Holy Scriptures. This fact makes the Bible not only necessary, but 'most necessary', since all those former ways of God's revealing his will to his people have 'now ceased' (cf. *The Westminster Confession of Faith*, chapter I, paragraph 1).

To summarize: What is the meaning of the fact that revelation has ceased?

It is not that God is dead and no longer communicates with people. The heavens still declare the glory of God, and the firmament displays his handiwork. The Holy Spirit who lives in every believer illumines the truth of God as found in Scripture, and applies it constantly to life and conscience. The Bible embodies God's personal selection of the special revelations he determined that the church would need through all the ages. In this written revelation from God is contained all that is needed for life and godliness. No further words, ideas, or supposed visions and prophecies shall supplement the completed revelation of Scripture. It is not just that the written canon is closed, meaning that no more words are to be added to the Bible. The end of revelation means that all those former ways of God's making his will known to his church have now ceased.

2.   THE HISTORY OF THE CESSATION OF REVELATION

At first blush, the idea of a 'history' of the cessation of revelation would appear to be a strange concept. It would seem more sensible either to affirm that revelation came to its end once and for all, or that revelation continues indefinitely. But if you commute to work each day, you know the meaning of stops and starts that continue until you arrive at your destination. At more points than you would like, you cease your progress due to a red light or jammed traffic. Though you make a definitive stop when at last you reach your goal, you have stopped and started all along the way.

In a similar way, God's revelation to his people involved a series of stops and starts along the way until it reached its destination in the person of Jesus Christ. From the very first stage of God's making known his will to his people, it was made clear that revelation was not a thing that would continue in an unbroken line as the experience of God's people. Instead, the revelation of the 'rule' [the canon] for the life of God's people was to be guarded as a distinctive phenomenon marked off clearly from other experiences that might occur throughout their lives. The reception of new revelation was not to be a part of their everyday, moment by moment experience. Instead, it was to be special, even as the collected revelation from God received at specific junctures generally is called 'special' revelation. Several considerations point in this direction.

a. *The 'Do not add' Declarations*
This history of the cessation of revelation has a very pointed introduction by the use of the phrase 'Do not add' when the collection of authoritative, inspired writings was first being formed. Generally it is presumed that the 'canon', the collection of inspired, authoritative utterances of God, came to its conclusion only when the New Testament had been completed. But from the beginning it was made plain that revelation would have various stages at which it was to be considered complete or finalized.

One of the first of these instances is found in the book of Deuteronomy, the inspired document that confirmed the covenant God made through Moses. After reiterating the ten commandments (*Deut.* 5:6-21), Moses notes that even God himself 'did not add' any further words. Instead, he had the ten words, the words of the covenant, engraved on two tablets of stone (*Deut.* 5:22). This distinctive treatment of the ten commandments sets them apart as having a unique role in the purposes of God. Never would any word be added to them. In so far as a summary statement of the moral will of God is concerned, the ten commandments brought the revelation of his will to its completion. Not a word would be added, not even by the Lord himself.

A similar statement is made concerning the whole of the revelation concerning the Mosaic covenant and its law-code. After tracing the history of God's dealings with his people from Sinai to the commissioning of Joshua in the plains of Moab (*Deut.* 1:6-3:29), Moses admonishes the people regarding the laws he is about to declare to them. He says: 'Do not any of you add to the word which I am commanding you, and do not subtract from it; but keep the commands of the Lord your God which I am commanding you' (*Deut.* 4:2).

Right then and there Moses was in process of delivering the authoritative commands of God to the people. As the prophet among his brothers, he was bringing to them the authoritative word of God. But even though Moses himself referred to the long sequence of prophets who would succeed him (*Deut.* 18:18), he now declares that no one must add to or subtract from the commands he is now delivering. In so far as the Mosaic covenant as summarized in the book of Deuteronomy is concerned, the 'canon' is closed. No further words are to be added to it.

So from this early declaration of Moses, the first writer of sacred Scripture, it becomes clear that revelation was not to come in unbroken continuance. Instead, it would come in units according to the progress of redemption. The people of the old covenant were not strangers to the idea of a 'closed canon'. They understood that authoritative laws for God's people came by revelation from God, and that no man must ever presume to add or to take away from that revelation. The idea of a completed body of revelation was as old as Moses, the first of the prophetic figures of the old covenant.

This admonition not to add or subtract from the authoritative revelation of God is repeated a third time in Deuteronomy 12:32. As enumerated in the Hebrew Bible, this verse actually serves to introduce the treatment of the subject of false prophets in Deuteronomy 13, rather than an isolated verse concluding Deuteronomy 12. Moses says: 'See that you do all that I command you. Do not add to it, or subtract from it' (*Deut.* 12:32, NIV). Having declared the exclusiveness of the revelatory words that he brings to them, Moses warns of the danger of false prophets in their midst (*Deut.* 13:1-18). These false prophets may be able to perform (false) wonders among the people, and the words they say may appear to come to pass. But if they summon the people to follow other gods, they must not be obeyed. For nothing is to be added or taken from the covenantal words spoken to Moses.

Once more it is clear that revelation will not come in unbroken continuance. Instead, further revelation will come as the history of redemption moves toward its consummative goal in Jesus Christ. Nevertheless the people of God learned early what it meant to be guided by completed units of revelation, even as they progressed toward the finalized revelation that was to be found in Jesus Christ. Receiving new revelation was not to be regarded as an experience that continued perpetually within the historical progress of God's people. Instead it came in spurts as God determined the time was right to introduce a further stage of revelation.

This understanding of the 'Do not add' passages in Deuteronomy provides the key to an even earlier statement at the time the Lord first indicated his intent to distribute the prophetic gift broadly among his people. During the wilderness wanderings, Moses found the people too heavy a burden for him to bear alone. The Lord commanded that he assemble the congregation. Then he took from the Spirit that was on Moses and put it on the seventy elders. The rabbis explain that this distribution of the Spirit was like the lighting of many candles from one. Moses' experience of the Spirit of God was not in the least diminished by the distribution among the seventy. But the effect of this distribution of the Spirit of revelation was made evident instantly. For when the Spirit rested on them, all the seventy elders 'prophesied' (*Num.* 11:25). Each elder became the source of a divinely inspired prophetic word. In a great rush of his Spirit on men, the Lord multiplied the revelational utterances that were available to his people.

But then the finalizing statement is immediately introduced: 'But they did not add' (*Num.* 11:25b). This phrase has been a puzzlement to interpreters, partly because of the abruptness of its introduction. But in view of the usage of this identical phrase in the passages in Deuteronomy previously noted, the meaning seems apparent. The seventy elders did not continue indefinitely in their proclamation of revelatory words. The prophetic speaking that they did for God was limited. It did not go on indefinitely. The Lord rounded out the revelation he intended to convey through the seventy elders, and then 'they did not add'. From the beginning of the outpouring of the prophetic Spirit, the point was made quite clearly. Revelational utterances would not proceed in a line of unbroken continuance. God's word would be completed in so far as each stage of his redemptive work was concerned, and at that point no one was to add to the revelation.

It is in this context that the uniqueness of the last 'Do not add' admonition of the Bible is to be understood. When almost the very last word of the Bible ends with a 'Do not add', it should be obvious that the Apostle John has a unique perspective on the concept. Moses the first writer of inspired Scripture introduces the idea of a completed revelation with his repeated 'Do not add'. Now John the last writer of inspired Scripture concludes the authoritative words of God with a summarizing 'Do not add':

> I bear witness to all who are hearing the words of the prophecy of this book: If anyone adds to them, God shall add to him the plagues written in this book; and if anyone takes away from the words of the book of this prophecy, God will take away his part in the tree of life and the holy city which are written in this book.

(*Rev.* 22:18-19)

There is a uniqueness to this 'Do not add' found in the last verses of the last chapter of the last book of the Bible. All the previous prohibitions indicated a rounding out of the revelation related to a particular phase of the progress of redemption. At the same time, they were anticipating a future 'end' of revelation that would come when the goal of redemptive history had arrived. Those earlier inspired units of God's inerrant word had the characteristics associated with the shadows, types, forms and images of the old covenant that demanded further revelations in the future. Though true in all their essences, they could only offer a foretaste of the glorious revelation that would come.

But now the aged John, appropriately regarded as the last survivor of the apostolic band, writes of the glories of the Christ not only as he saw him on earth, but as he was privileged to see him in heaven. Here now is the ultimate vision of the glorified Son of God to be experienced by man in his present state. Of this final revelation of Christ, the goal of all revelation, nothing is to be added to it and nothing can be subtracted from it. Any modification of this his splendour, any subtraction from this his glory will have eternal consequences. All the awesome curses of John's final revelation of the future will fall on the presumptuous one who dares even to attempt to add to his glory. For fallible human efforts to supplement his honour by their imagined insights can only pervert the perfections of this inspired, authoritative picture of the glorified Christ.

This final 'Do not add' obviously applies first to the book of Revelation written under God's inspiration by the Apostle John himself. To the prophecy of this book nothing is to be added, and from the book of this prophecy nothing is to be taken away. But the book of Revelation holds a unique position in the authoritative revelations from God. Presenting Christ as he will be seen again only when he returns in glory, its admonition that no one must presume to add excludes any and all pretensions to further revelations.

In this regard, the uniqueness of this present era must be appreciated fully. It is not like any other period in redemptive history that has preceded. All periods before Jesus Christ's ascension to glory at the right hand of the Father were preliminary. By the very nature of the case, those previous revelations from God demanded, expected and received a fuller revelation that would make them complete. But now the end of this long process has come. Now the goal has been manifested in its fullest glory, so far as the present age is concerned. It is for this reason that it cannot be argued that further revelations in the present era would only conform to the pattern of previous eras, and would not detract from the completeness of the revelation in Scripture. This era is unique in that the Son of God himself has finally come. Any claims to add further revelation beyond the end of God's word as it is found in the completed Scriptures would be not only superfluous but blasphemous. For it could only diminish the glories of the glorified Son of

God. As revelation could not be complete before Christ came, so it could not be incomplete after he came.

It is true, we wait for the final *apokalupsis*, the last unveiling of the Son of God that shall bring an end to this present era. At that time every eye shall see him in all his splendour. But so far as the present age is concerned, the full manifestation of the significance of his person and work comes clearly through the inscripturated, authoritative Scriptures of the Old and New Testaments. To them no one must presume to add upon peril of his soul.

The 'Do not add' admonitions of Scripture indicate that the idea of a cessation of revelation is not a strange concept in the process of God's working of redemption for his people. Revelation never came as an unbroken experience. The previous cessations anticipated the conclusion of revelation that came with the consummation of the revelatory process as it was realized at the incarnation of the very Son of God.

b. *The 'End' in Relation to the 'Means' of Special Revelation*
The repeated cessations of revelation which we have considered go along with the nature of special revelation as a means to an end and not an end in itself. In contrast with the expectation that all the members in Christ's church will bring forth the fruit of the Spirit as a part of their continuous, unbroken experience, no such expectation may be attached to the experience of Christ's church with respect to the gifts that bring new revelation. This principle is brought out clearly in the extended discussion of Paul regarding the 'gifts' of the Spirit in relation to their goal or 'end' as found in 1 Corinthians 13.

What is the 'end' or goal of revelation according to Scripture? Objectively, the goal of God-given revelations is found in the person of Jesus Christ. He is the alpha and the omega, the first and the last, the beginning and the end, the yea and the amen of all the promises of God as they have been revealed throughout history. In Jesus Christ the object toward which all revelation points is realized in its fullness. Subjectively, the goal of all revelation is identified by Paul as love. Because God is love, because all God's will for men is summed up in the two commandments of love, the goal of revelation must be found in the formation of love in the recipients of divine revelation. Paul makes exactly this point when he declares: 'Where there are prophecies, they will cease; where there are tongues, they will be stilled; where there is [the communication of new revelational] knowledge, it will pass away' (*1 Cor.* 13:8b).

But the abiding character of love is set in sharpest contrast with the cessation of these gifts related to revelation. For as the Apostle says, 'Love never fails' (*1 Cor.* 13:8a). Abounding in all the extraordinary gifts that bring revelation means nothing apart from love (*1 Cor.* 13:1-2). Speaking in the tongues of men and angels, possessing the gift of prophecy that involves the understanding of all divine mysteries, exercising miracle-working faith that moves mountains — the manifestation of all these revelational gifts means absolutely nothing if a person does not participate in the point of them all, which is the experience of love.

But just as these miraculous gifts had a temporary function in the life of the individual who experiences them, so they also had a temporary function in the life of God's people as a whole. The fruit of love should be a vital part of the life of God's people all the time. But the miraculous gifts of prophecy and tongues enter into the experience of God's people spasmodically, and ultimately passed away. Once the objective goal of God's revealing himself to men in the person of Jesus Christ had come, then no need remains for a continuation of new revelations. While subjective experience in the growth of love will continue throughout the present era, further revelation of Jesus Christ the object of love will progress no further once his glories have been made evident.

For this reason, the 'fruit' of love must be seen as more excellent than the 'gifts' of prophecy and tongues. As Jonathan Edwards states so well: 'When the Spirit of God is poured out for the purposes of producing and promoting divine love, he is poured out in a more excellent way than when he is manifested in miraculous gifts.'[1]

It was so easy for the spectacular gifts to dazzle the church, to draw its gaze from the more modest manifestations of love in a person's life. But the Lord's people must be instructed by his word. Paul says a person gains nothing and is himself nothing if his concentration is on the gifts of the Spirit rather than on the fruit of the Spirit.

The distinction between the 'means' and the 'end' of revelation can go a long way toward curing this imbalanced perspective in the church. Concentration must be directed toward continual growth in the 'fruit' of the Spirit above interest in the 'gifts' of the Spirit. Since the 'goal' of revelation has been realized in the coming of Christ, God's people must not continue looking for gifts that would communicate new revelation. In accepting this new state of things, the people of God should not mourn out of a sense of loss because of the end of the special gifts of revelation any more than the children of Israel should have mourned when the manna stopped as they entered the land of Canaan. They had arrived at their goal! They were in the land flowing with milk and honey! They had the advantage of a full feast from the produce of the land! Should they begin moaning because they had to plow in the morning rather than simply collect the manna? There were, after all, real advantages related to the manna in the wilderness over the produce of the land. Manna was present in adequate supply every morning without fail. But would it have been appropriate for the Israelites to complain over the cessation of the manna because of the work involved in fulfilling God's command to 'subdue the earth' once they had entered the land of promise?

The church's relation to the miraculous gifts may be paralleled to Israel's experience with the manna. Should the church complain that the miraculous gifts of tongues, prophecy and the ability to work wondrous signs have ceased as a result of the coming of the consummate revelation in the person of Jesus Christ? Obviously not. It would be nothing but childish immaturity for God's privileged people today to complain about the cessation of the spectacular means to the end when the end itself has arrived.

It is important, then, that the church distinguish between the means and the end of revelation. If this distinction can be grasped, and the superiority of the end over the means fully appreciated, then the church will not constantly be 'looking over its shoulder' to the 'good old days'. Then the church will be ready to revel in the riches that are found in the person of Jesus Christ himself. As Paul stresses with young Timothy: 'The end of the commandment is ... love out of a pure heart and unhypocritical faith' (*1 Tim.* 1:5).

c. *Evidence of the Decline of the Revelational Gifts in the New Testament Era*

The silence of four hundred years between the Testaments sets a backdrop of 'negative space' that only enhances the brilliance of the explosion of new revelation that came with Christ's appearance. But within this, the greatest era of revelation from God, certain signs and structures anticipated the end of new revelations. Gradually attention was focused on a completed 'canon' solidifying the inspired interpretations of the significance of Christ's coming. Two phenomena found in the new covenant Scriptures point specifically in that direction: the pattern of the manifestation of the gifts of prophecy, tongues and miraculous signs in Acts; and the contrast between Paul's earliest and last writings as they relate to the subject of the end of revelational gifts.

i. The Pattern of the Manifestation of the Gifts of Prophecy, Tongues and Miraculous Signs in Acts

The programmatic text for the book of Acts is found in Jesus' words to his disciples just before his ascension into heaven. They must be his witnesses in Jerusalem and all Judea, in Samaria, and to the uttermost parts of the earth (*Acts* 1:8). In three distinctive concentric circles, the witness about Jesus must be taken to the world. First in the essentially Jewish community of Jerusalem/Judea, then to the Samaritan community toward the north, and finally to the vast Gentile world that stretched to the distant unknown isles. Only and precisely by following this procedure would the will of the risen Christ be fulfilled. When this was done, it would be done. All the basic phases of the task would have been achieved when the testimony had expanded through these various territories.

Stimulating studies have analysed the entire structure of Acts according to this pattern of ever-enlarging areas where the gospel would be preached.[2] Even the geographical designations specifically indicated in the programmatic statement of Acts 1:8 appear to be followed intentionally through the book. Beginning in Jerusalem (*Acts* 2), proceeding to Samaria after the martyrdom of Stephen (*Acts* 8), advancing to the Jewish/Gentile borders in Palestine with the baptism of Cornelius at the seacoast Caesarea (*Acts* 10), the book ends with Paul in Rome after having made three sweeping trips across the expanses of the Gentile world. Luke concludes his narrative at that point because the programme of expansion as described in the first chapter of his book had reached its outer limits.

Beyond the end of the book of Acts, it would be only more of the same. Until the consummation, the spread of the gospel would not involve the introduction of a new stage in redemptive history, but only a further extension within the realms already reached by the witness.

Strikingly, Luke's reporting of the manifestation of the gifts related to new revelation tracks this same pattern of advance. First, in Jerusalem the gift of tongues is manifested (*Acts* 2:4). Everyone hears the witness concerning the mighty acts of God in their own 'tongue' or 'language' (*Acts* 2:6). Then in Samaria, great signs are worked by Philip, and the people receive the Holy Spirit when Peter and John lay their hands on them (*Acts* 8:13, 17). It is not specified that the people in Samaria manifested the gift of tongues. But the context in Acts strongly supports this conclusion. For Simon 'sees' that the Holy Spirit has been given, which suggests physical phenomena that would compare with the experience of Pentecost (*Acts* 8:18). Next, Peter is summoned to Caesarea, thirty miles up the coast from Joppa, where the Holy Spirit descends on all the Gentiles that hear him preach. Peter cannot see how baptism can be denied, since they already have demonstrated that the Spirit had come on them by their 'speaking in tongues' (*Acts* 10:44-48). The apostles are still in Palestine, but now it is Gentiles who have received the Holy Spirit, manifesting gifts related to new revelation. Finally, the 'uttermost parts of the earth' are represented by the baptism of the Spirit on the believers in Ephesus (*Acts* 19:4-7). Paul declares to them the name of Jesus, and as they are being baptized, the Holy Spirit descends and they speak in tongues and prophesy.

Accordingly, the manifestation of the gifts of prophecy and tongues in Acts coincides exactly with the stages and phases of the advance of the gospel as set out in the programmatic verse in the opening chapter of the book.

In Jerusalem/Judea, in Samaria, and to the uttermost parts of the earth the work of the Spirit has been manifested. When the book of Acts ends, all the principal stages involved in the advance of the gospel have been realized. Obviously much more will have to be done before the gospel has been proclaimed fully to all the nations. But the further history of the spread of the Christian gospel may be regarded as an extension of the last stage of the proclamation to the world as described in the book of Acts.

The externalized display of the gifts of the Spirit indicated the sanction of the Lord on each of these new stages of advancement. Not at every point were these revelational gifts experienced by the church. Instead, the programmatic structure of Acts explains the pattern of the manifestation of these extraordinary gifts: first in Jerusalem/Judea, then in Samaria, and finally to the uttermost parts of the earth.

This programmatic structure not only defines the pattern of the display of the gifts of tongues and prophecy in Acts. It also provides a rationale for an end of the experience of the revelational gifts. As the gospel passes from Judea to Samaria, the confirming gifts are manifested. Then once more as the gospel crosses over massive barriers and enters into the vast world of the Gentiles the manifestation of these extraordinary gifts confirms the blessing of God. Since no further distinctive stages of advancement are left in the processes of redemptive history, no further externalized manifestations of the extraordinary gifts of the Spirit should be expected.

The pattern of the manifestation of the gifts related to new revelation therefore provides a rationale for the cessation of these particular gifts of the Spirit. Once the process of advancement has come to its final stage, no need exists for a continuation of the confirmatory gifts.

ii. The Contrast Between Paul's Earliest and Last Writings

Further evidence regarding the decline of the special revelational gifts in the New Testament era may be seen in the contrast between the earliest writings of Paul and his last writings. Paul's interest in the revelational gifts that provided the foundation for the church of the new covenant is quite evident. This personal interest on Paul's part underscores the significance of his testimony in this area.

Paul's initial letter to the Thessalonians very likely is the first inspired writing of the New Testament era. So it should not be surprising at all to find the Apostle admonishing the church: 'Despise not prophesyings' (*1 Thess.* 5:20). Four hundred years of revelational silence had preceded the dawning of the days of the new covenant. But now suddenly prophetic utterances are both current and manifold. It might be expected that these new prophetic words from the Lord would run into some resistance. Paul therefore employs his apostolic authority to instruct the church that it should not despise this new manifestation of the revelational gift of prophecy. Instead, it should be viewed as a proper manifestation of the working of the Spirit accompanying this new stage in the history of redemption.

The Apostle also recognizes the validity of the revelational gifts of prophecy and tongues in his early letters to the Roman and Corinthian churches. If a person has received the gift of prophecy, he should exercise that gift (*Rom.* 12:5). One and the same Spirit is the source of gifts of healing, performing miracles, prophesying and speaking in tongues (*1 Cor.* 12:9, 10).

As is generally recognized, it is in his first letter to the church at Corinth that Paul offers his fullest discussion of the gifts of tongues and prophecy (*1 Cor.* 12-14). In these chapters it becomes evident that these extraordinary gifts are being exercised broadly in Corinth, so much so that their use must be carefully regulated (*1 Cor.* 14:29-33). To establish his right to speak on this subject, Paul indicates that he himself speaks in tongues more than any of them (*1 Cor.* 14:18).

The Apostle's interest in the role of these particular gifts takes a significant turn in the letters written during the middle days of his career. He speaks in Ephesians of the 'apostles and prophets' as the foundation on which the church is being built (*Eph.* 2:20). He refers to the revelation concerning the nature of the church that has been made known to 'God's holy apostles and prophets' (*Eph.* 3:5). He speaks of those whom Christ appointed to be apostles and prophets, along with evangelists, pastors and teachers (*Eph.* 4:11). While these particular offices are seen as still functioning in the church, they are being presented as providing a foundation of revelation on which the church as a whole can be built.

But the level of interest in the gifts of tongues and prophecy declines dramatically in the last writings of Paul. In his first letter to Timothy, the gift of prophecy is not mentioned except with reference to the prophecy that had been uttered earlier at the time of Timothy's ordination (*1 Tim.* 1:18; 4:14). The gifts of tongues and prophecy are nowhere mentioned in Titus or 2 Timothy, except for the mention of the prophetic revelations constituting the Scriptures of the old covenant (*2 Tim.* 3:16).

What has happened? Is it to be concluded that these gifts related to new revelation still were functioning widely at this late date in the apostolic age, since no command forbidding them has been issued? The precise opposite would seem to be the case, particularly in the light of Paul's extensive remarks regarding a phenomenon that appropriately could substitute for the unending continuation of these revelational gifts. In his last letters to Timothy and Titus, Paul employs a number of phrases underscoring the importance of holding to the sound teaching that has been provided them. Titus is told that an elder in Christ's church 'must hold firmly to the trustworthy message as it has been taught, so that he can encourage others by sound doctrine' (*Tit.* 1:9). The erring must be rebuked sharply, 'so that they will be sound in the faith' (*Tit.* 1:13). Titus himself is charged to teach 'what is in accord with sound doctrine' (*Tit.* 2:1). In a most forceful way, young Timothy is charged to 'keep as the pattern of sound teaching' the things he has heard from Paul (*2 Tim.* 1:13). He must 'guard the good deposit' that has been entrusted to him (*2 Tim.* 1:14), referring to the doctrines he has been taught. Envisioning a development that stretches across four generations, Paul (the first generation) admonishes Timothy (the second generation) to entrust to reliable men (the third generation) who can teach others also (the fourth generation) the teachings he has received from the Apostle (*2 Tim.* 2:2). Timothy must show himself to be a good workman, rightly handling the word of truth (*2 Tim.* 2:15). He must beware of men who as far as the faith is concerned are rejected (*2 Tim.* 3:8). In reflecting on the nearness of his end, Paul notes that he has 'kept the faith' (*2 Tim.* 4:7).

These many references to an established body of doctrine in 2 Timothy and Titus point to a different circumstance than that which was addressed in Paul's earlier writings. The complete absence of reference to the gifts of prophecy and tongues in these later letters contrasts radically with the circumstance prevailing in the earlier correspondence with the Thessalonian, Corinthian and Roman churches. Now the Apostle is concerned to make provision for the church's ongoing need for the truth in the future. Along with the other apostles, he will soon be gone. He locates God's provision for the future not in an ongoing experience of the special gifts of tongues and prophecy, but in the established revelation that has been provided during the years of the apostolic age. There is 'the deposit' of truth, there is 'sound doctrine', there is 'the tradition', there is 'the faith', there is the 'trustworthy message'. It is not that there was no awareness earlier of a 'deposit' of faith, a body of doctrines to be believed, for reference can be found in Paul's earlier writings to this kind of phenomenon (cf. *2 Thess.* 2:15; 3:6). But the completeness, the sufficiency of a tradition of teaching that had been received came only at the end of the apostolic age.

All of this evidence points to the formation of a body of truth recognized as having come by revelation from God. This revelational material would provide the divine inter- pretation necessary for the church to understand properly the redemptive events associated with the coming of Christ into the world. Before any inspired Scriptures of the new covenant had been provided to the church, the revelational gifts of prophecy and tongues were being exercised exten- sively. Partly as an expression of the fullness of the blessings of God's Spirit as he was poured out in the new covenant era, partly as an experience designed to meet the church's need for revelational understanding of the new day into which it was entering until the new covenant Scriptures could be formed, these gifts of revelation at first were in abundant manifestation in the church.

But Paul's stress at the end of his life on the importance of holding fast to the doctrine, the tradition, the faith that had been revealed provides a different picture altogether. A process has been completed, an era has come to an end. The church should not expect that new revelations will continue forever to interpret the significance of the coming of Christ into the world. Instead, the body of doctrine re- ceived by revelation will become the guide for the life of the new covenant church.

So the New Testament provides significant evidence of the decline of the revelational gifts. The history of redemption unveils a process of revelation that finally provides a completed body of doctrine that will serve to instruct the church until the end of the present era. That body of doctrine naturally finds its completeness in conjunction with the work and teaching of the apostles and their immediate companions, those who were eyewitnesses of Christ in his glory, and were the recipients of his special commission to provide the foundation for his church throughout the succeeding ages.

3.   OBJECTIONS TO THE CONCEPT OF THE CESSATION OF REVELATION

God's 'final word' to his people is found in Jesus Christ and in the inspired explanations of his person and work as preserved in the old and new covenant Scriptures. While most professing Christians are quite comfortable affirming the uniqueness of the person of Jesus Christ, many find it difficult to accept the concept that no further revelation is to be expected as guidance for their lives other than that which is found in Scripture. Objections to the idea of the cessation of revelation come from a number of considerations.

a. *Scriptural Objections*
The first objection to the idea of an end of the functioning of the revelational gifts today arises from the perception that this assertion directly contradicts specific biblical injunctions. The Apostle Paul declares, 'Despise not prophesyings' (*1 Thess.* 5:20). Even more pointedly he states, 'Do not forbid to speak in tongues' (*1 Cor.* 14:39). Who would presume to stand against these God-inspired injunctions and tell people that they cannot either prophesy or speak in tongues?

Hopefully no person who affirms the authority of the

Bible would have the audacity to oppose any biblical injunction. Certainly it would not make sense to resist specific biblical commands when the intent is to affirm that the Scriptures contain in themselves the fullness and finality of divine revelation. But the question is not whether prophecy and tongues should be forbidden by men. Instead, the question is whether prophecy and tongues have been brought to their completion and their end by the plan and purpose of God.

It is a fact that cannot be denied that some divine injunctions have bound the people of God for a particular era, but have subsequently been revised, modified or even cancelled. Obviously many commands given in the Old Testament no longer bind God's people today. Despite the clear biblical prohibition, it is all right to boil a kid in its mother's milk. A person living under the age of the new covenant is not defiled by eating pork or oysters. These commands, though clearly divine in their origin, no longer determine the lifestyle of God's people.

The same principle holds for some commands in the new covenant era. Phases and stages in the development of the new covenant may not be as dramatically different from one another as in the case of the old covenant periods. Yet differences clearly exist. At one point Jesus sent his disciples out and told them to take no provisions with them (*Luke* 10:4). Later he gave them virtually the opposite instructions (cf. *Luke* 22:36. At one stage he explicitly forbade them to go to the Gentiles; they must limit themselves to the 'lost sheep of the house of Israel' (*Matt.* 10:6). But later he commanded them to go into all the world and make disciples of all nations (*Matt.* 28:19). As a result of the decision at the Jerusalem council, the word was sent forth forbidding all the churches to allow its members to eat things that had been strangled or polluted by idols (*Acts* 15:20). But later Paul declares that God has made all foods clean and that offering a piece of meat to an idol has no effect on its eatability so long as a weaker brother is not led into sin (*1 Cor.* 8:4, 9).

More closely related to the present concern is the cessation of the office of apostle in the church. Nothing in Scripture explicitly indicates that the apostolate ever would come to an end. Yet it generally is recognized that no one in the church today functions with the authority of the original apostles, since no one today has been an eyewitness of his resurrection (*Acts* 1:21-22).

If it is recognized that the apostolic office has come to an end, then the possibility must be acknowledged that the foundational office of prophet also has ceased to function in the church today. This office, after all, is listed as second in priority only to the position of the apostle (*1 Cor.* 12:28). Furthermore, the office of prophet throughout the ages served as the principal vehicle through which revelational materials were communicated to God's people. Since the institution of the prophetic office in the days of Moses, God regularly spoke to the fathers through the prophets (*Heb.* 1:1). If the offices of apostle and prophet have come to their end in the church today, it would be natural to conclude that the revelational utterances of apostles and prophets also have ceased. No current pronouncements bearing apostolic authority give direction for the church. In the same manner, it would be natural to expect that with the end of the prophetic office has come the end of revelational words delivered by the prophets.

With respect to tongues, it obviously would be wrong to forbid a person to speak in tongues, if it were the case that the modern phenomena actually were the same as New Testament tongues. No amount of shock that might be caused in a traditionalized church could justify the exclusion of this gift from the public worship service, if the tongues of today were the same as the tongues of the New

Testament. Paul's admonition clearly intends to stop all efforts to exclude the exercise of a legitimate gift of the Spirit among God's people.

But on the other hand, if the tongues of today are not the same as the tongues of the New Testament, then clearly a person would not be violating Paul's injunction if he refused to allow someone to speak at a worship service in a mode that was something other than New Testament 'tongues'. The proper elements for worshipping God must be limited to those exercises commended in his word, since men have no right to invent their own way of approaching the Almighty. If the tongues of today are not the same thing as the tongues commended by Paul, then it would be quite appropriate to exclude them from the worship service.

These biblical injunctions not to despise prophecy or to exclude tongues apply to the worship circumstances of today only if modern-day 'tongues' and 'prophecy' are identical with the Spirit's gifts as they functioned in the days of the apostles. If the current phenomena are not the same as the New Testament gifts, then it would be quite appropriate to forbid their exercise in the worship of God's people.

b. *Theological Objections*

Several objections of a theological nature may be raised against the affirmation that revelation and the gifts related to new revelation have ceased. These objections largely may be placed in three categories:

i.   It is objected that a blanket assertion that revelation has ceased today has the effect of limiting God. Is it proper to restrict God by saying that he cannot communicate by revelation directly with someone today if he chooses? Would it not be rather presumptuous under any circumstances to limit God? Of course. It would be quite presumptuous for any man to presume to limit God. No man has the power or the authority to restrict God in any way. Yet a time-worn tool for instructing children may offer a significant insight into this matter. The Catechism for Young Children asks, 'Can God do anything?' The answer contains a certain profoundness that even the most sophisticated adult should appreciate: 'Yes, God can do all his holy will.'[3] If God has chosen to reveal himself according to a certain pattern, it is not limiting God to affirm the Lord's own design in this matter. If he determines that it is best to bind his people together by requiring that they seek his will from a single source objectively known to them all, is it for man to propose that he shall make his will known through thousands of different individual sources separated by time and space from one another?

It is not limiting God to say that miracle-working as depicted in the New Testament occurs no more today, if God himself has determined that these signs attesting Christ and his apostles have served their purpose by confirming once and for all the foundational truth necessary for the ongoing life of Christ's church. His mighty works among men today are obvious at every hand. But his continual working in the world of today does not necessarily imply that he intends to continue miraculous activities related to new revelations. No man can limit God. It would be both blasphemous and presumptuous to attempt to restrict the Almighty. But faith in him will not hesitate to affirm that he will act consistently in accord with his own declared intentions.

ii. It is objected that the pagans of today have need of the confirming power of signs, wonders, prophecy and tongues just as much as did the heathen of the first century. Why should men today be denied revelational experiences that could be instrumental in bringing them to saving faith? But once more, the pattern established in the Lord's own word must take precedence over hypothetical suppositions devised by men's imaginations. Is it true to Scripture to say that the extraordinary gifts of prophecy, tongues and miracles had their principal manifestation among the heathen who had never heard? Or is it not closer to the facts as recorded in Scripture that miraculous signs occurred instead among those who already had been identified as God's people?

Yes, the heathen were startled by Paul's shaking the poisonous snake into the fire without his being harmed by its bite (*Acts* 28:3-6). Yes, the church at Corinth may be characterized as a predominantly Gentile church in which tongues served as a sign to unbelievers who attended their assemblies (*1 Cor.* 14:22). But it was at the assemblies of God's people that these gifts were manifest, not among the heathen who had not heard. The overwhelming evidence points to the fact that gifts of a revelational nature functioned most extensively among established churches confirming God's will among his people rather than as wonders worked in the eyes of the world.

It is the proclamation of the truth that makes sinful men free. An evil and an adulterous generation seeks to base its faith on the miraculous rather than on the truth of God plainly spoken (*Luke* 11:29). The Holy Spirit does not need miracles to convince men in their hearts of the truth of God's word, and we should not think that he does.[4] A strong faith in the power of the gospel's truth will go much further toward the salvation of sinners than a reliance on the miraculously dazzling. The established pattern and the explicit teaching of Scripture is that the clear proclamation of the truth rather than the working of wonders is the most effective method for spreading the gospel.

c. *Practical Objections*

One further category of objections to the end of revelation needs to be noted. It is objected that in the practical realm it is not wise to deny the continuation of revelation. Many people strongly believe that God has communicated with them. A great number of dedicated servants of Christ regularly recount visions that have led them to commit their lives to Christ. Is it then practical to conclude that these people have suffered from an illusion? Could it not be harmful to the body of Christ to deny that God has been revealing himself in these extraordinary experiences?

With all due respect, it may be quite practical to lead people to 'test the spirits' to see whether they be of God or not. What one person calls a 'vision' actually may have been a moving application by the Holy Spirit of the truth of Scripture to his life. Someone may be functioning in exactly the right place of service in Christ's kingdom, though he got there by a very dubious path. One of the most dedicated, happily married elders serving in Christ's church testifies that he determined to marry his wife by letting his Bible fall open and putting his finger on a verse! As has been well said, God is quite capable of 'striking a straight blow with a crooked stick.'

It is a very practical thing to lead people to recognize the finality of revelation in Scripture. Many a young believer could be saved from serious heartbreak if he learns to trust the objective teachings of the word of God more than his own sense of having received a 'revelation' from the Lord. Responsible decision-making never will be learned by God's people so long as they think they must wait for God somehow to 'reveal' his will to them before they can act.

Chapter Four

Current Advocacy of the Continuation of Revelation

Throughout the history of the church some people have looked for the continuation of special revelation from God to provide direction for their lives. The Romanists have looked to church councils and the pope, while the mystics have looked to the inner voice. The higher life movement has looked to 'feelings' communicated by the Spirit, and others have looked to a 'word from the Lord' through contemporary prophecies.

Men seem to have great difficulty being content with an objectively recorded word from the Lord which binds them to basic religious principles while simultaneously freeing them for responsible decision-making. A person wants to avoid the personal responsibility of determining to sell his house and relocate his family, so he 'puts out the fleece' as a way of getting a contemporary 'word from the Lord' that relieves him of the risk involved in making a mature decision himself. Someone may intend to divorce his spouse on a basis that is not found in the written word of God, so he looks for some extra-biblical 'message' that will give him the freedom to do what he wants.

Other more noble motivations may move people to seek a fresh word from the Lord — not one that will contradict Scripture but that will speak more directly to the present hour. Personal loss may drive a person to cry out for something that speaks more specifically to his situation than the words of a psalm or a chapter from the book of Revelation. Uncertainty about making a marriage commitment or going to the mission field may seem to require a confirmation that comes more directly than a verse taken from one of Paul's epistles, as helpful as scriptural formulations may be.

The Reformers who paid with their life-blood for freedom from dominance by the traditions of the church were especially jealous in guarding future generations from the oppressions created by supposed words from the Lord. 'Scripture alone' was their uncompromising cry. Only the written Word of God, an objective standard which all men can see and read, communicates infallible truth to God's people, since God now has stopped using his former methods of revealing his will to the church (*Heb.* 1:1). But the search goes on for a new way for God to continue revealing his will in ways other than through Holy Scripture. Each new generation offers a slightly different twist on the recurring theme.

The current drift in this direction has been formulated well in a work by Wayne Grudem entitled *The Gift of Prophecy in the New Testament and Today.*[1] This work comes with highest commendations from respected contemporary evangelical scholars. It offers to unite the vitality and insight of modern-day Pentecostalism with the doctrinal stability inherent in the churches that came out of the Reformation. A new view of 'prophecy' is proposed that intends to provide a fresh approach to the way God communicates his will to the church today. This new view of prophecy has found significant acceptance in large areas of the evangelical church. Its promise to revitalize staid worship services of earlier days has been readily accepted by a growing constituency.

Yet large problems arise from this approach to prophecy.

The assertions of this viewpoint offer a serious challenge to the finality of revelation as it is found in Christ and the Scriptures. Several points in this regard must be noted.

1.   THIS VIEWPOINT ASSERTS THAT REVELATION CONTINUES TODAY

This view boldly and unequivocally contradicts the assertion that revelation has ceased. The point is repeated often. It is affirmed that 'a revelation from the Holy Spirit' is 'essential to prophecy' (p. 135). It is stated that 'Paul assumes that all who prophesy have received a "revelation"' (p. 137). Because the prophet Agabus described future events, his predictions must be 'based on something that had been revealed to him' (ibid). The point is summarized in terms that cannot be mistaken: 'A "revelation" from the Holy Spirit is necessary for a prophecy to occur. If there is no such revelation, there is no prophecy' (p. 139).

This unequivocal affirmation that revelation continues in conjunction with prophecy is qualified by a number of conditions. It even may appear to be contradicted by the stress laid on the point in the opening pages of the book that 'prophecy' which is delivered today is not to be regarded as equivalent in authority to Scripture (pp. 14f.). To resolve the tension between belief in continuous revelation and the finality of Scripture, Dr Grudem argues that the 'reception' of a revelation by a prophet is only the first ingredient of the current prophetic experience. According to this new perspective on prophecy, the next step in the process must be the delivery of the revelation by the prophet to the parties concerned (p. 139). Grudem believes that while a revelation may be given 'for the private benefit of the individual recipient', it only falls into the category of a 'prophecy' when it is delivered to others (ibid). And it is at this point of delivery of the prophetic message, his argument goes, that human error invariably enters into the picture, because the full authority of the revelation given from the Lord is diluted when transmitted to others by the prophet. As we shall see, Grudem seeks to prove that this type of fallible, 'ordinary congregational prophecy', which he alleges continues today, already existed in the New Testament era. Its exercise depends upon revelation from God but the pure Word of the Lord is corrupted by factors of human error.

In its major distinctives, this position on continuing revelation through prophecy must create serious problems for the Christian today. Prophecy as uniformly presented in Scripture refers not merely to a revelation received by an individual. Most importantly, it is the speaking of the very Word of God to the people that marks the work of the prophet. Prophetic words were in themselves the revelation of God to the people. But this new position proposes that the delivery of the prophetic message is flawed by the human instrument, even though a pure revelation came originally to the prophet.

At the same time, this position contradicts unequivocally the viewpoint that holds that revelation ceased at the end of the apostolic age when the authoritative writings of the New Testament were completed. The Reformers did not declare simply that no new writings were to be added to the Bible. They stated instead that all those former ways by which God made his will known to his people now have ceased. Whether it be by dream, vision, theophany or prophecy, all those former ways of God's declaring his will to his church came to their conclusion when the significance of Christ's coming was fully explained through the New Testament Scriptures.

This new proposal has serious consequences for the life of the church. It creates an extremely unstable environment for the people of God with respect to the identification of 'a word from the Lord'. Nothing could be more crucial for God's people than a clear understanding of what God has said regarding his will for their lives. Yet this view creates serious ambiguity at the very point where clarity is imperative.

Prophecy is extolled by Grudem as being superior to all other gifts of the Spirit (p. 153). This superiority is said to arise from the fact that divine revelation to the prophet uncovers the specific needs of the moment which may be known only to God (ibid). A preacher can depend only on his own personal observations to determine the specific needs of an individual or a group. But because prophecy is based on divine revelation about the current situation of the church which is communicated directly from God, the prophet can speak pointedly to the specific needs of the moment at the precise time when the congregation is assembled (p. 152). In many cases 'the things revealed' to the prophet might include 'the secrets of people's hearts', 'their worries or fears', or 'their refusal or hesitancy to do God's will' (ibid).

The significance of a prophet's speech on the basis of this kind of revelational knowledge that supposedly comes immediately from God might best be comprehended if it is viewed from a personal perspective. Right then and there in the middle of the worship service, a respected and godly person addresses you as an individual and declares your 'refusal ... to do God's will', and demands that you do what he says you should. What would be the effect of that kind of experience? God's word for your personal life has come to you from a person that has received a revelation about you directly from God. Would it not rest as the heaviest of burdens on you to do exactly what you had been told?

But wait! There is a cloud, an element of ambiguity that remains. According to this perspective on prophecy, the instructions that come from a prophetic utterance 'should not be considered divine obligations' (p. 167). Instead, they should be viewed as 'the prophet's own fairly accurate (but not infallible) report of something he thinks (though not with absolute certainty) has been revealed to him by God' (ibid). So if you choose to disobey the admonition of the prophet, you might not be disobeying God, for you heard only the fallible representation of the Lord's prophet.

But what if the prophet who received this revelation got the message mainly right when he addressed you? It would be disobeying God for you not to do what the prophet said. How can it ever be positively affirmed that a person is not disobeying God if he fails to do what the prophetic utterance declares? Is a revelation from God really of such little consequence, even if reported in a fallible form? Why would God bother to reveal something to a prophet if he did not expect the recipient of the prophet's message to do what he said?

While prophecy in this view clearly is 'superior to the other gifts' (p. 153), and specifically better than teaching or preaching because it is based on a revelation from God concerning the immediate situation in the church (p. 152), yet teaching based on the written Word of God has 'far greater authority than occasional prophecies which the speaker thought were from God' (p. 145).

Can you sense the instability that would be created in the lives of God's people by this dubious approach to New Testament prophecy? On the one hand, prophecy is said to be based on a revelation that comes directly from God, uncovering the truth about persons or situations that otherwise could not be known. But on the other hand, these revelations are delivered by the prophet in such a garbled manner that the person addressed may choose to ignore them altogether if he wishes. For it is stated that even those who are not quite sure if they have received a revelation should be encouraged to go ahead and speak out in the manner of a prophet, since that is probably what Paul would have done (pp. 147, 211). But to take the confusion even one step further, God might even 'cause words to come to mind which he does not want us to take as his own words' (p. 121).

Perhaps this last assertion should be repeated so that its full significance may be grasped. According to this new view of prophecy, God might even *'cause words to come to mind which he does not want us to take as his own words'* (p. 121, italics added). How could anything be further from the biblical concept of prophecy? What could contradict more radically the nature of the God of all truth? Would he have a prophet serve as his spokesman and yet cause words to come to the prophet's mind that he himself does not want the people to consider as his words? No, God is not the author of such confusion.

* * * * * * * * *

To understand more concretely the puzzling relation now alleged to exist between revelation and prophecy, let it be supposed that a prophet delivers a word to the congregation based on a revelation he has just received. He reports as a prophetic utterance, as has been hypothetically proposed: 'You should marry Philip' (p. 167). Is it to be supposed that somehow the prophet has become confused and the person addressed actually should marry David instead of Philip? Or has the prophet addressed his word to one person when actually it should have been directed to her sister? Or was it that the person addressed was to go out to dinner with Philip (or was it David?) rather than marry him (or him)? What is the point of it all if the prophet is going to get the message so confused that a person cannot tell what to do? Why would God bother to give a revelation and then design a manner of communication of his message that is so confusing that no one can really tell exactly what he did or did not say, not even the prophet himself?

Or suppose that God reveals to a contemporary prophet that the world's economy will worsen for the next three years. This revelation from the Lord the prophet delivers to the congregation. Only he gets slightly confused and says the recession will last two years instead of three. How will the congregation judge this prophecy? To what biblical verses shall they appeal to test its authenticity? Jesus did say that famines would come in the end time, and that men's hearts would fail them because of their worrying over troubles on the earth (*Luke* 21:26). If some Christian economists in the congregation agree that the forecast of a two-year recession seems reasonable, shall the members of the congregation be encouraged to sell their stocks and shares while they have a high value? And if the economic track over the next two years appears to confirm the prediction, shall the congregation again be advised to buy back into the market, assuming the recession now will bottom out? What a disaster it would be if the recession actually lasted for three years rather than two. What recriminations might be hurled against prophet and preacher if people lost significant savings. Yet it all could happen on the basis of good faith that God wanted to protect the assets of his people so they could use them for the advancement of his kingdom.

God is not the author of such confusion. He would not put his people into such a precarious position in which they could not determine his will on a matter concerning which he had revealed himself. This concept of prophecy has the potential for creating great uncertainty in the lives of God's people. For on the one hand, the word of the prophet is said to be based on a revelation from God, and so demands all respect and honour. But on the other hand, this word from the prophet is said to be polluted by contact with fallible human agents and so it is unworthy of the confident trust of God's people.

It might be proposed that this situation is no worse than the circumstance brought about by a specific application of the Bible that might come from an ordained minister of God's Word. But the two situations are drastically different. In the case of an admonition addressed to the congregation by a preacher or teacher, the basis of the teaching is immediately available to the congregation. Each member of the church can search for himself the same Scriptures as their teacher, and are admonished to do so. But in the case of the supposed 'prophetic' word, only the prophet himself has direct access to the revelation that came from God. The revelational basis of his prophecy remains his exclusive property. While the 'prophecy' may be subjected to a testing by Scripture to determine whether or not some outright sin would be involved in heeding the prophet's commands, it clearly is not the same thing as having immediate access to the revelational words themselves which are the basis of the supposed prophecy.

As a consequence, this view of prophecy has the potential for creating great confusion among the people of God. Except for comparing with the general maxims of Scripture, no way exists for judging objectively whether or not a prophetic deliverance actually has come from God.

In addition, this kind of 'prophecy' seriously threatens the freedom of conscience of the individual Christian. Because these supposedly prophetic words would appear to be much more directly applicable than the general maxims of Scripture, they would tend to interfere with the freedom of the Christian to make his own decisions about how his life ought to be lived in obedience to God. If in the middle of the worship service you were told by a prophetic utterance that you should sell your home and move to another part of the country, and this word were supported by other respected members of the congregation, what would remain of your freedom to determine between you and the Lord what you ought to do? Even if that freedom formally might be granted by the group, the pressure certainly would be strong for you to submit to the 'prophetic word'.

In this regard, the ambiguity of attitude toward prophecy becomes quite apparent. Several charismatic spokesmen are quoted as indicating that prophecies which tell a person what to do in specific circumstances should neither be accepted nor rejected. They should be kept in a 'pending' file until confirmed in one way or another (pp. 246f.). Yet prophecy is said to be 'superior to the other gifts' (p. 153). Because it is based on a revelation directly from God that speaks specifically to an individual's current situation, it is claimed as superior to teaching and preaching. But if a prophetic word has that kind of superiority, how can a person remain comfortable in his own conscience while not doing what it says?

Even though questions about the divine origin of a 'prophetic word' may be raised, what if this prophetic utterance actually is the very Word of God specifically to an individual regarding a concrete circumstance? Because of this supposed origin of contemporary prophecy in a revelation directly from God, the freedom of the conscience of the individual believer would be challenged continually by these prophetic utterances, whatever caveats might be appended.

In view of these practical problems, what is the appeal of this current view of prophecy? Why should a person be willing to risk supplanting the certainty of Scripture for the ambiguity of fallible prophetic utterances? Why would anyone be open to the possibility of surrendering his freedom of conscience in favour of subjugating himself to a supposed word from the Lord? Clearly this view of prophecy appeals to the human thirst for a sense of immediacy in a person's relationship to God. The 'living presence of the Lord' is the benefit offered by this view of prophecy (p. 148).

This view also appeals to the democratic spirit of the day. People like the idea of the 'town hall' meeting in which everyone is equally free to offer his own observations, whether profound or otherwise. With this view of the role of prophecy in the church, everyone can anticipate that he will have the opportunity to offer his own contribution to the worship of the church. All will have the freedom to speak according to the moving of the prophetic Spirit (p. 147). The church's message will not be restricted to the pronouncements of a few trained clergy. Instead, anyone and everyone will have the freedom to speak openly in the assembly.

These appeals must not be overlooked, since they may be rooted in genuine needs of the body of Christ. But these considerations must not be allowed to displace the stability arising from seeing the Scriptures as the only source of divine revelation to men. All the needs of God's people will be answered to the fullest as the church follows the prescriptions of the Scriptures themselves. Rather than constricting the regenerated spirit of the saint, the ordering of God's Word will liberate him to serve the Lord to the fullest.

2. THIS VIEWPOINT HANGS ON AN EXEGETICAL STRING

In a religion based totally on special revelations from God rather than on fallible judgments of men, perfection in the material that brings the divine revelation is a foundational necessity. Otherwise the will of God for his people forever will remain a matter of uncertainty. If uncertainty characterizes the delivery of the word from the Lord, then inevitably the lives of God's people will manifest the same kind of ambiguity.

This foundational principle is seen clearly in the insistence on perfection in the revelation that comes through the prophets of the old covenant. Though their words came in the shadowy forms of old covenant images and types, every word they spoke had to be the very Word of God. No admixture of error could be tolerated. Death was the sentence that must be executed on a prophet whose deliverances contained a single utterance including error.

Essential to the view currently under discussion is the proposal that prophecy in the congregations of the new covenant is of a different sort. Although based on an infallible, inerrant, divine revelation that comes to the prophet, the actual utterances of the prophet's mouth invariably contain errors introduced in the process of transmission. In this regard, 'ordinary congregational' new covenant prophecy is treated as though it were of a different sort than old covenant prophecy.

This alleged difference between old covenant and new covenant prophecy could not be more basic. It may be compared to the difference between the view that finds errors in the Bible and the view that sees the Scriptures as containing only the infallible, inerrant Word of God. The evangelical community of God's people has consistently affirmed that a revelation from God that contained error would be a misleading guide to God's people. Yet now within the evangelical community has arisen this view that genuine revelations from God present themselves to the people in a fallible form.

If the new covenant in every way is 'better' than the old, it rightly could be expected that every part of the new covenant would be better than its old covenant counterpart. Christ on the cross is better than the brazen serpent on a stick. Resurrection from the dead is better than exodus from Egypt. Baptism is better than circumcision, and inheriting the new heavens and the new earth is better than possessing Palestine. In this context of comparisons between the old covenant and the new, it would seem strange indeed if new covenant prophecy took on a form that was significantly weaker in manifesting divine perfections than its old covenant counterpart. Obviously the content of new covenant prophecy is far more glorious than old covenant prophecy. But is it to be expected that this more glorious reality is to be communicated through a fallible, unreliable form of prophecy in drastic contrast with the unbroken perfections of 1500 years of old covenant prophecy?

Certainly it could be expected that if this kind of change in the nature of prophecy were to occur, a clear word from the Lord would forewarn God's people. Prophecy from Moses to Christ had been an embodiment of the very words of God, absolutely reliable in every syllable. If now under the new covenant it were to take on the form of fallible, human utterances, as this current position affirms, it might be expected that God would clearly, unequivocally indicate this drastic change in the nature of prophecy.

Yet the whole argument for the inferior nature of new covenant prophecy hangs on an exegetical string. The scriptural arguments put forth to support this radical denigration of the divine institution of prophecy simply cannot bear the weight of the assertions being made. Consider first of all the arguments based on the teaching concerning prophecy found in 1 Corinthians, which form the principal core of the case for a different kind of prophecy than that which was experienced under the old covenant.

a. *Arguments for an Inferior Kind of Prophecy Based on the Teaching about Prophecy in 1 Corinthians*

i. 1 Corinthians 14:29

No other verse is referred to more frequently in this discussion than 1 Corinthians 14:29. Regularly, appeal is made to the statement that 'two or three prophets should speak, and the others should weigh carefully what is said' (NIV). Particularly the last phrase, 'weigh what is said', is appealed to as indicating that prophecy as experienced in Corinth could not have been of the same sort as old covenant prophecy. How could the prophecies at Corinth have the character of infallible, unquestionable utterances that embody the very words of God if the congregation must 'weigh carefully what is said', determining what elements of the prophecies are correct and what elements are to be treated only as the opinions of men?

Let it be clear from the outset that the entire argument based on this verse hangs on an exegetical string. It builds on inferential wording that actually is not even found in the Word of God. The words '(weigh) what is said' are not to be found in the original text of Scripture, but have been added by translators as their interpretation of the passage. Not a single ancient manuscript of the New Testament contains these words. The full significance of this fact must be noted. A principal exegetical argument for a different kind of prophecy, a fallible prophecy whose 'good' elements must be separated from its 'bad', arises from wording that is not found in Scripture. Nine of the twenty-one pages in Grudem's book that deal with prophecy in 1 Corinthians are given over to the treatment of this single verse. A dozen times in these pages he makes reference to the phrase '(weigh) what is said', indicating the significance in his view of these words that have been inserted by the translators. The argument favouring a different kind of new covenant prophecy rests heavily on an appeal to words that do not even exist in the New Testament!

Of course, the addition made by the NIV translators was intended as an interpretive remark but there is a far better way of interpreting this phrase in 1 Corinthians 14:29. The verse reads literally, 'Two or three prophets should speak, and the others should discriminate' (*diakrino*). As pointed out earlier, this term is frequently used in the New Testament to refer to a discrimination among people, not words or ideas. Peter says that God made no discrimination between Jewish and Gentile believers in the outpouring of the Holy Spirit (*Acts* 15:9). Paul asks the rhetorical question of believers at Corinth, 'Who made you to differ from anyone else?' (*1 Cor.* 4:7). Again he asks, 'Is there nobody among you wise enough to discriminate among his brothers?' (*1 Cor.* 6:5). James expresses concern that his fellow Christians have 'discriminated among themselves' by making a difference between the rich and the poor (*James* 2:3-4). In these passages, three different New Testament authors use the term *diakrino* to indicate a distinction between people, not between words or ideas. It is worth noting that two instances of this use of the term are found in the first letter of Paul to the Corinthians.

In the context of 1 Corinthians 14, Paul is not concerned with a new kind of prophecy in contrast with the old covenant variety. He is concerned instead about a new abundance of prophecy, which is exactly what Joel's words as cited at pentecost anticipated (*Acts* 2:16-18). With all this abundance of words from the Lord, the church must be careful to see that all is done decently and in order, for God is not a God of disorder but of peace (*1 Cor.* 14:31-33). All who have a prophetic word from the Lord eventually will have the opportunity to prophesy, but the spirits of the prophets must remain subject to the prophets.

It is precisely in this context of the discussion of church

order as it related to the exercise of the prophetic gift that Paul says: 'Two or three prophets can speak, and the others must discriminate' (1 Cor. 14:29). The 'others' to whom Paul refers would appear to be other prophets who have the same gift as the ones bringing the prophetic word, although the reference could be to the rest of the congregation. But in any case, the 'discrimination' appears to involve a determination about who will speak, and in what order. As we have already seen, the words 'weigh carefully what is said' do not even appear in the text of Scripture and involve an unnecessary inference.

The argument that this phrase in 1 Corinthians 14:29 introduces a new kind of prophecy that includes error along with truth is based on a flimsy exegetical foundation. It builds on inferential wording not found in the original text of Scripture. It does not harmonize with the context of 1 Corinthians 14, in which Paul is explicitly developing principles for order in the church rather than discussing a new kind of prophecy in contrast with the type that had prevailed for the previous 1500 years in the experience of God's people.

ii. Other arguments from 1 Corinthians

In a summary statement concerning the teaching of 1 Corinthians regarding this proposal of a legitimate kind of new covenant prophecy that would contain error, Grudem makes five points (p. 87). Once again, the tendentious character of these proposals may be observed. In three of the five cases, he indicates that it 'seems' that his conclusions can be properly reached. This kind of qualification indicates the uncertain character of these various arguments that supposedly are establishing a new kind of prophecy in the new covenant era. A closer look at these arguments underscores the uncertainty of the case being made.

Firstly, it is argued from 1 Corinthians 14:29 'that the prophet's words could be challenged and questioned, and that the prophet could at times be wrong' (p. 87). Already it has been indicated that the phrase '(weigh) what is said' does not appear in the original text of Scripture, and that the context as well as the usage of the word 'discriminate' suggest instead that the judgment involved a decision as to who among the prophets would speak. But even if the 'discrimination' envisaged were related to the words spoken by the prophets, nothing in this procedure would distinguish new covenant prophecy from the prophecy of the old covenant. For judgment was rendered regularly about the true or false character of the words spoken by a 'prophet' in the old covenant (cf. *Deut.* 13:1-5;18:21-22).

The new covenant documents clearly anticipated the presence of false prophets. Christ himself warned about the many false prophets that would work themselves into the fellowship of God's people (*Matt.* 7:25; 24:11, 24). Paul later speaks of false apostles that were troubling the church at Corinth (*2 Cor.* 11:13, 26). Peter and John also recognize the troublesome character of false prophets in their day (*2 Pet.* 2:1, *1 John* 4:1).

In the light of this widespread expectation concerning the presence of false prophets within the new covenant community, the proposal that 1 Corinthians 14 should be read as envisioning error within legitimate new covenant prophecy rather than as anticipating the possibility of false prophets within the church of Corinth builds precariously on an argument from silence. The proposal that the assumed error appears in legitimate new covenant prophecy rather than in false utterances which are not genuine prophecy is an exegetical argument that hangs on a string. The absence of any mention of 'false' prophets in 1 Corinthians 14 hardly provides a basis for establishing a new kind of legitimate prophecy in the new covenant community, a prophecy that contains error mixed with truth. Recognizing that judgments had to be made concerning new covenant prophecies does not in itself distinguish this kind of prophecy from old covenant prophecy. Clearly this recognition would not in itself indicate that legitimate new covenant prophecy 'could at times be false' (ibid). For the utterance would not actually be a prophecy from the Lord if it proved to be false.

Secondly, it is argued that new covenant prophecy as represented in 1 Corinthians 14:30 is different from old covenant prophecy because Paul 'seems unconcerned that some of a prophet's words could be lost for ever and never heard by the church' (p. 87). This conclusion is based on a particular understanding of the effect of an interruption of one prophet by another before the first prophet had completed the delivery of his message. But this picture of the situation at Corinth appears to be based more specifically on contemporary experiences of 'prophecy' in a modern charismatic context than on an evaluation of the actual evidence provided by Paul. Is it clear that the only prophetic revelations experienced by the church in Corinth came spontaneously during the worship service? Does Paul anywhere exclude the possibility that some prophetic revelations may have come days or even weeks before the public assembly at which they were delivered? Would not this possibility explain why a more urgent revelation that came during the worship service might be allowed to interrupt a less urgent prophecy? And does Paul anywhere suggest that the prophet who had been interrupted could not later arise to complete his prophetic deliverance? What Paul explicitly says is that although things must be done decently and in order, all of the prophets eventually will be given a full opportunity to deliver their word from the Lord (*1 Cor.* 14:31). The whole idea of a lesser kind of prophecy in which some words never would be heard by the congregation hangs by a string of suppositions rather than on clear exegetical evidence.

Thirdly, it is argued from 1 Corinthians 14:36 that since Paul by his rhetorical question denies that the word of God has come from the Corinthians, their prophets must not have the same authority as the old covenant spokesmen. But once more the tendentious character of this interpretation of Paul's words is apparent. Does Paul actually state that the prophets of Corinth did not deliver the word of God? Is he not instead denying that the word of God had its origin among them, as represented in several current translations? It is further supposed from this verse that the Corinthians could make no rules for the conduct of their worship other than what Paul had delivered to them (p. 85). Yet the verse simply says, 'Did the word of God originate with you? Or are you the only people it has reached?' (*1 Cor.* 14:36). It is hard to derive from these rhetorical questions that Paul is denying that the Holy Spirit has communicated divine revelations through their prophets. As a matter of fact, the opposite conclusion would make much greater sense. The word of God has as a matter of fact reached them as well. It is just that they are not the only ones who have been the recipients of divine revelations.

Fourthly, it is insisted that the prophetic word at Corinth was inferior to the Apostle's words since the Corinthians are denied the right to compete with Paul's authoritative words. Paul states that anyone in Corinth who thinks he is a prophet must recognize that the thing Paul writes is a command from the Lord (*1 Cor.* 14:37). Since by this statement Paul requires the prophets at Corinth to recognize the apostolic authority of his writings, it is concluded that the prophets at Corinth could not speak authoritative words

103

from the Lord as did the apostles.

But once more the conclusion greatly strains the evidence. To say the prophets at Corinth could not contradict Paul is not quite the same thing as saying they could not supplement Paul. Obviously no word from the Lord will contradict a previous word. But denying the Corinthian prophets the right of contradiction is not the same thing as denying them the right to speak a fresh word from the Lord. If the establishment of the existence of a different kind of prophet who has less authority than the old covenant prophets rests on this kind of argumentation, it depends on a weak foundation.

Finally, it is argued that since Paul allows women to prophesy but not to teach authoritatively in the church, the prophetic utterances of the new covenant could not have the authority of their old covenant predecessors. But once more the argument is not compelling. A different explanation makes far greater sense of the exegetical evidence. A prophet was purely and simply an instrument, an organ of the word of God. Heathen Balaam could serve as the Lord's prophet because of the purely instrumental nature of the prophet's function. But the office of an elder or teacher could not be filled by someone like Balaam. This role of responsibility hinged on a person's ongoing exercise of authority over the congregation, supported by the testimony of his own life. Without reflecting on the Christian character of women, Paul under the inspiration of the Holy Spirit denied to them the ongoing exercise of authority over the congregation embodied in the office of elder because of the order established by God at creation. But he would not deny that a woman might serve as an appropriate instrument of prophetic revelation to God's people, even as they had done under the provisions of the old covenant.

In sum, these various arguments from 1 Corinthians for an inferior kind of prophecy do not have a great deal of strength. A multiplication of the number of inferential arguments does not in itself strengthen a case being argued. In exegesis as in mathematics, zero plus zero plus zero equals zero. In contrast with Dr Grudem's effort to denigrate 'ordinary congregational' new covenant prophecy, the clear language of 1 Corinthians speaks repeatedly and explicitly of a 'revelation' that comes through new covenant prophecy (*1 Cor.* 14:26-31). Someone might assert that the 'revelation' to which Paul refers describes the communication of the Lord to his prophet, while the delivery of the word to the congregation ends up being something less than a revelation. But this assertion needs to be established by unambiguous exegetical evidence, particularly in the light of the established significance of prophecy all along the history of God's people that had preceded this point in time. Prophecy always had been the supreme mode by which God communicated his will to his people. In their uniform experience, the prophet's words were the very words of God. Not so much in typology or even in theophany but through prophecy God communicated his will to his people (cf. *Heb.* 1:1).

Furthermore, 'prophecy' in Scripture describes first and foremost a process of speaking forth, not of internal reception. The term itself focuses on the delivery of a message, not the reception of a message. If revelation is associated with prophecy, the first assumption would be that the 'speaking forth' of the message constitutes the 'revelation'. Sometimes the prophet might receive his revelation prior to its delivery. But at other times the delivery of the revelation would be simultaneous with its reception by the prophet; the prophet's mouth did not move by mindless impulses, yet no time-gap or mind-gap existed between the reception and the delivery of the revelation.

In any case, the burden of proof must rest on the person proposing a dichotomy between the prophet's reception of a word from the Lord and his delivery of an authoritative revelation, contrary to the consistent experience of the old covenant messengers for as much as 1500 years. In light of consistent biblical usage, terms other than 'prophet' ('spokesman') and 'prophecy' ('message') would have been far better if the intent of Paul in 1 Corinthians were to describe a situation in which a 'revelation' would come from God to an individual but his reporting of the revelation would be something less than the very word of God.

1 Corinthians is the single book among new covenant documents that develops most fully the picture of prophecy in the community of the new covenant. Yet the case for a different kind of prophecy than that which had been experienced previously among the people of God hangs on an exegetical string. Suppositions based on inferences hardly can provide adequate justification for this kind of radical alteration of the pattern of God's revelation by his prophets through all previous ages.

b. *The Evidence of the Rest of the New Testament*

i. The analysis of evidence from Acts in Wayne Grudem's *The Gift of Prophecy in the New Testament and Today* begins with Acts 11. Yet the critical link between old covenant prophecy and its new covenant counterpart appears in Acts 2 as it records the experience of Pentecost. Peter orients the events of that great day directly to Joel's 'prophecy about prophecy'. The classic old covenant experience of prophesying, seeing visions and dreaming dreams is equated with the occurrences of the day of Pentecost by the phrase 'this is that' (*Acts* 2:16). Peter equates new covenant prophecy with its old covenant equivalent. Miraculously the apostles have been given the power to prophesy in all the languages of the people assembled at Jerusalem.

If, with this starting-point, the intent of the book of Acts is to develop a different kind of prophecy for new covenant congregations, it might be expected that some sort of explicit indicator of a change in the nature of prophecy would be provided along the way. Yet no such indicator exists. As a matter of fact, between Acts 2 and the explicit mention of the utterance of a new covenant prophecy in Acts 11, repeated reference is made to the holy prophets of the old covenant who spoke the Word of God infallibly and inerrantly (*Acts* 2:30; 3:18, 21-25; 7:37, 42, 48, 52; 8:28, 30, 34; 10:43). Having set in place that kind of biblical background, the report is given of prophets that come to Antioch from Jerusalem. One of them named Agabus 'predicted that a severe famine would spread over the entire Roman world' (*Acts* 11:28). In view of the consistent testimony of the nature of prophecy in Acts up to this point, and considering that it would have been absolutely impossible for Agabus to have known about a famine of the future apart from divine revelation, it seems clear that the 'prophecy' being experienced in this new covenant setting is exactly the same as the prophecy of old covenant days.

Yet it is argued that the 'vagueness' of the words reporting the prophecy of Agabus suggests a lesser kind of authority than the normal prophetic word (p. 90). It is stated that the word for 'predicted' (lit. 'gave a sign') as used in secular Greek literature refers only to a 'vague indication of what is to happen' (ibid). What more could be expected from secular prophets attempting to describe the future, we may ask, without the advantage of divine revelation? How could they possibly offer anything but a 'vague indication' as they attempted to guess what would happen in the future?

But did Agabus give no more than a 'vague indication' when he 'predicted through the Holy Spirit' that a severe

107

famine would spread through the entire Roman world? The term for 'predicted' of necessity may have had a vagueness attached to its use in secular Greek. But an analysis of the term as it is used in the New Testament strongly reinforces the idea that the words of Agabus were inspired prophetic predictions just as much as any old covenant prophecy. The Greek word translated 'predicted' occurs five times in the New Testament outside Acts 11:28. In four of these five instances the term clearly describes prophecies about the future that by the nature of the case must have been infallible, inerrant utterances having the full authority of God's inspired word. Jesus himself 'predicted' the kind of death he was going to die when he spoke about his being lifted up (*John* 12:33). The Jews later demanded Christ's crucifixion as a fulfilment of the words of Jesus when he 'predicted' the kind of death he would die (*John* 18:32). Obviously these uses of the word indicate prophecies that must be as fully authoritative as the God-inspired predictions of the Old Testament. 'That it might be fulfilled', the principal formula in the Gospels indicating the fulfilment of an Old Testament prophecy, is applied to this 'prediction' of Christ.

The words of Jesus that 'predicted' the kind of death by which Peter would glorify God have the same significance (*John* 21:19). Is it to be proposed that the words of the risen Christ that anticipate the future death of his disciple had a 'vagueness' that made them less authoritative than the utterances of the old covenant prophets? No less authoritative was the revelation of Jesus Christ that God gave the apostle John which enabled him to 'predict' to his servants the things which were soon to take place (*Rev.* 1:1). Certainly the prophetic 'predictions' of the glorified Christ as communicated to John and recorded in the book of Revelation had no less authority than the prophecies of the old covenant.

This identical term describes Agabus' 'prediction' of the coming famine. The word suggests no 'vagueness' or 'lesser kind of authority' (p. 90) than the previous prophetic words introduced in the New Testament by the same word. The prophecy of Agabus fits exactly the pattern of prophecies from the Old Testament mentioned in the earlier chapters of the book of Acts. Though not an apostle, the prophet Agabus predicts the future with full divine authority. The indication that he spoke 'through the Holy Spirit', far from suggesting 'a rather loose relationship between the Holy Spirit and the prophet' (p. 90), confirms the fact that he was the instrument of divine revelation to men. The proposal that the Greek preposition 'through' in the phrase 'through the Holy Spirit' indicates 'a rather loose relationship between the Holy Spirit and the prophet, since it allows room for a large degree of personal influence by the human person himself' (ibid) stretches the force of the Greek preposition beyond reasonable propriety. The broadly varied significances of this Greek preposition make it highly inappropriate to be used as a basis for a precise significance which would outweigh contextual considerations as well as the other uses of the term 'predict' throughout the New Testament.

As the book of Acts proceeds with its record of the spread of the gospel, it notes the continuation of the manifestation of the gift of prophecy. Both in Antioch (*Acts* 13:1-2) and at Ephesus (*Acts* 19:5-7) reference is made to the exercise of this gift in the church. No indicator is given, explicitly or implicitly, that a new kind of prophecy has now been introduced into the life of the church. On the contrary, Acts 19 deliberately echoes the experience of the church at Pentecost when the prediction of Joel about widespread prophecy found its first fulfilment in the community of the new covenant. Twelve apostles originally prophesied in all the different languages of the people assembled in

Jerusalem. Now in Ephesus, when the gospel is being proclaimed 'to the uttermost parts of the earth', twelve men
speak in tongues and prophesy. In view of the total absence
of any indicator that this prophesying was different from
what happened at Pentecost, and in the light of the seem-
ingly deliberate parallelism in the description, it may be
concluded that the prophesying that occurred in Ephesus
was the same as the prophesying that occurred in Jerusalem. On the day of Pentecost, Joel's prediction concerning
the widespread manifestation of the gift of prophecy found
its first fulfilment, and the only kind of prophecy that Joel
knew to predict was the kind that had been experienced
since the days of Moses. This same prophecy of Joel finds
further fulfilment by the coming of the prophetic Spirit on
the twelve men at Ephesus.

The statement that the prophesying at Ephesus 'bears
no resemblance to the messenger speeches in the Old
Testament' (pp. 92-93) is an assertion made without sub-
stantiation. The fact that a number of people prophesied
hardly supports this assertion, particularly in the light of the
experience of Pentecost. Nothing in the text supports the
unfounded assertion that the prophesying at Ephesus 'does
not seem to have been of the type which possessed the
absolute authority of God's very words' (p. 93).

The strongest case for a different kind of prophecy in the
new covenant community may be derived from the prophecies related to Paul's going up to Jerusalem. In its baldest
form, Acts 21:4 indicates that 'through the Spirit' the
disciples at Tyre urged Paul not to go on to Jerusalem. Yet
earlier Paul reported to the saints in Ephesus that
he was 'compelled by the Spirit' to go to Jerusalem (*Acts*
20:22). On the surface of things, it appears that the report
of an apostle regarding the work of the Spirit is flatly
contradicted by the urging through the Spirit that comes
through the disciples. This way of putting things captures

the issue quite well. Is it to be concluded that the true nature of new covenant prophecy now has become clear? Is it
that through one and the same Holy Spirit messages are to
be delivered to God's people for their direction that flatly
contradict one another?

Several noteworthy commentators of various theological
persuasions have no problem resolving the apparent discrepancy. Neither Johannes Munck nor F.F. Bruce nor J.A.
Alexander nor John Calvin suggests that the Spirit has contradicted himself, or that New Testament prophecy hereby
is proven to be a mixture of good and bad, of truth and
error. Each in his own way concludes that the Spirit revealed to these disciples the sufferings Paul would undergo
at Jerusalem. To this perfected revelation the concerned
disciples appended their own conclusion: that Paul should
not proceed to Jerusalem. It was not that the Spirit or
prophecy erred at this point. Instead, it was simply that the
disciples' concern for the well-being of their mentor limited
their apprehension of the good that might come from
Paul's suffering for Christ's sake. As Calvin so aptly sum-
marizes the matter: 'it is no marvel if those who excel in the
gift of prophecy be sometimes destitute of judgment or
fortitude.'[2]

Strong confirmation of this explanation of the apparent
conflict of messages from the Holy Spirit is found in the
immediately succeeding narrative. When Paul and his
travelling party arrive at Caesarea, the Spirit speaks once
more. This time the prophet Agabus is his instrument.
Agabus prophesies that in Jerusalem Paul will be mal-
treated both by Jews and Gentiles (*Acts* 21:10). Luke
specifically includes himself and Paul's other travelling
companions along with the people of Caesarea in the spon-
taneous response to this solemn message of the prophet:
'When we heard these things, we in consort with those who
lived in that place exhorted him not to go up to Jerusalem'

(*Acts* 21:12). The language of their exhortation is virtually identical with the phraseology of Acts 21:4, 'that he should not go up (over) to Jerusalem'. But now the context is spelled out more fully. Agabus the prophet follows precisely the pattern of his old covenant counterparts. First he enacts the predicted event by binding himself with Paul's belt. Then he declares the message the Holy Spirit had revealed to him concerning Paul's afflictions when he arrives at Jerusalem. Out of concern for the apostle, everyone attempts to dissuade Paul from continuing on his way. When they realize they cannot change his mind, they resign themselves to what surely must come: 'The will of the Lord be done' (*Acts* 21:14).

This subsequent elaboration on the same incident provides the context in which the apparent conflict may be resolved between the work of the Spirit in compelling Paul to go to Jerusalem (*Acts* 20:22) and the message 'through the Spirit' from the brothers in Tyre urging Paul not to go to Jerusalem (*Acts* 21:4). The Spirit revealed the trials Paul would undergo, and the brothers took it on themselves to attempt to persuade him not to proceed. Is it that Paul 'simply disobeyed' the prophetic word that came from the brothers in Tyre? (p. 94). Does this passage establish a new kind of prophecy that comes 'through the Holy Spirit' and yet is erroneous and non-authoritative in the life of God's people? Can justification be found for disobeying this different kind of new covenant prophecy because of its inferior quality?

The issue is not simply a matter of semantics, an argument about using the term 'prophecy' to describe a supposedly erroneous word coming through the Holy Spirit. The issue instead is whether a justification can be found in this incident for the introduction into current worship practices of a different kind of prophecy than that which had been known for hundreds of years prior to this particular event. Shall the church on this basis allow an individual to interrupt the worship service to deliver a 'prophecy' that includes a mixture of truth and error if he claims to have received a 'revelation' from God that must be reported to the congregation? The evidence of Acts 21:4 does not provide adequate support for such an intrusion into the orderly worship of God. Prophecy continues in Acts to be an utterance with full divine authority. It was not an erroneous reporting of what a person thinks God might have said to him.

Further questions of a serious nature are brought out in conjunction with the prophecy from Agabus as reported in Acts 21:11. Grudem argues that at two points the prophecy is inaccurate: (1) the Jews did not bind Paul as Agabus said they would, and (2) they did not deliver Paul into the hands of the Romans (pp. 96f.). The point of this whole effort is to find some mistakes in this sample of non-apostolic new covenant prophecy so that the way can be cleared for a continuation of the same kind of inaccurate but legitimate prophetic activity in the church of today.

Two responses may be offered to this peculiar effort of a professed evangelical to uncover error in prophetic phenomena of the new covenant:

First of all, is it actually so clear that Agabus was wrong in his description of the events associated with Paul's arrest in Jerusalem? Twice it is reported that the Jews 'seized' Paul (*Acts* 21:27, 30). Is it so very clear that they did not 'bind' him as they seized him and 'dragged him from the temple' (v. 30)? In a similar way, is it actually so clear that the Jews did not 'deliver' Paul to the Romans as Agabus had predicted? The Jews seized Paul and were in the process of beating him when the Roman officials arrived at the scene (*Acts* 21:32). Is it to be insisted that there was no 'delivering' of Paul by the Jews as the Roman commander came up and arrested him? Must it be assumed that the

Jews totally relinquished their grasp on Paul before he was arrested by the Romans? The sketch of the tumultuous scene hardly tells the whole tale, and it is quite possible that things occurred exactly as Agabus predicted.

Secondly, care must be taken to avoid the trap of 'precisionism' in interpreting the prophecies of Scripture. Once a certain brand of preciseness in detail is demanded, difficulties of all sorts may arise. In its major thrust, the whole of Agabus' prophecy was fulfilled. The Jews were the instrument of the seizure of Paul which ultimately ended in his arrest by the Romans. That is the point of Agabus' prophecy. While on occasion the prophetic word of the Lord may manifest detailed preciseness, it certainly is not always the case. In an earlier chapter of Acts, Philip quotes Isaiah 53 as prophesying the sufferings of Christ (*Acts* 8:32-35). This prophetic chapter above all others in the Old Testament may be regarded as an accurate anticipation of the sufferings of Jesus. Yet in that chapter it is stated that the suffering servant of the Lord was assigned a grave with the wicked, and was with the rich in his death (*Isa.* 53:9). Yet according to the record of the New Testament his grave was with the rich and he was with the wicked in his death. Is it to be concluded that Isaiah the prophet erred in the details of his prediction? Or is it not of the nature of biblical prophecy that it is not precisionistic in its form? My point is not to prove prophecy under the old covenant to be in error. Instead, the point is to liberate the Scriptures from an unrealistic precisionism that does not characterize the Lord's word. The argument we have considered for a different kind of prophecy on the basis of supposed inaccuracies of new covenant prophecy is not convincing.

ii. Dr Grudem argues at great length that a distinction must be made between the authority of 'apostolic prophecy' and 'ordinary congregational prophecy' (pp. 25-65).

This argument simply stated is that Paul's references to 'apostles and prophets' in Ephesians 2:20 and 3:5 actually describe a single office, 'apostle/prophet', rather than two separate offices. It was this single office of 'apostle/prophet' that came to an end once the revelational foundation of the new covenant church had been laid. But another kind of prophet, it is said, the 'ordinary congregational prophet', continued to function after the apostolic prophets had ceased to exist.

This argumentation is necessary if it is to be posited that the office of prophet continues beyond the apostolic age. For if 'apostles' and 'prophets' as two separated offices shared the one-time responsibility of providing the foundational revelation for the new covenant church, then the implication is that both these offices ceased to function in the new covenant church once the foundation had been laid.

This new view willingly affirms that the office of apostle ended once the revelational foundation of the new covenant church had been completed. The discussion of Ephesians 2:20 and 3:5 even assumes that the office of prophet as mentioned in these passages came to an end with the completion of the foundation for the church. Yet somehow room must be made for the continuation even into the church today of a 'prophet' who continues to receive revelation from God. Otherwise the entire thesis that prophecy continues today falls to the ground. So the case must be made for two kinds of 'prophets' in the new covenant era. There were the prophets that were at the same time apostles, and there were the 'ordinary congregational prophets'. In this view it is the foundational kind of 'apostolic prophets' that ceased to function in the church, while 'ordinary congregational prophets' continue.

In order to establish this hypothesis, a lengthy case is made on the basis of detailed grammatical analysis that bears no weight of compulsion. To assert that 'apostle' and 'prophet' can be combined in Ephesians 2:20 and 3:5 because the definite article is omitted by no means indicates that they should be combined. Both in 1 Corinthians 12:28 and Ephesians 4:11 the two offices unquestionably are separated from one another by the use of the definite article in one case and the use of 'first' (apostles) and 'secondly' (prophets) in the other. The explicit separation of the two offices in the mind of Paul must certainly bear more exegetical weight than a mere grammatical possibility.

After almost twenty pages of argumentation on this point, the assertion is made by Grudem that even if two separate foundational, revelation-receiving offices were intended by the reference in Ephesians 2:20 and 3:5, 'it should not significantly affect the argument of the rest of this book' (p. 62). For he is then prepared to argue that the foundational 'prophets' of these verses were different from the 'ordinary prophets' scattered throughout the New Testament churches. So now the hypothesis has been expanded to allow for the possibility of three different kinds of new covenant prophets: apostolic prophets, revelational prophets, and ordinary congregational prophets. Yet no solid evidence can be cited to support such distinctions. This internal dialogue makes the author appear as though he has assumed what he intends to prove despite evidence that may point in a contrary direction. Obviously a person may assume that somewhere in the New Testament a clear distinction can be found between 'foundational' prophets and 'ordinary' prophets. But at some point this distinction must be established on an exegetical basis.

iii. Only one other passage requires serious consideration with respect to the proposal of a different kind of prophecy in the experience of the new covenant community. In the earliest of Paul's writings, a statement occurs which requires some consideration. The first letter to the Thessalonians concludes with a string of admonitions: 'Do not put out the Spirit's fire; do not treat prophecies with contempt. Test everything. Hold on to the good. Avoid every kind of evil' (*1 Thess.* 5:19-22).

Paul says that prophecies are not to be treated with contempt. Literally he states that they must not be regarded as though they were nothing. Why would the apostle feel compelled to give this kind of directive? What kind of situation should be envisaged in which prophecy is at risk of being treated as nothing? This admonition makes good sense in the light of the early date of Thessalonians in the development of the new covenant community. For four hundred years the prophetic gift had not functioned. The written Torah had been the only source of revelatory data in the life of God's people for centuries. It is quite reasonable, then, that the new community of believers would be extremely suspicious of claims that new revelations were coming in the form of contemporary prophetic utterances. Their natural inclination might well have been to treat them as though they were nothing. In their minds, contemporary prophecy did not exist. So Paul instructs them in this element of the newness of the new covenant era. They should expect that fresh words from the Lord will come through prophetic instruments, just as they came in the days of the old covenant. Only then would they be able to comprehend the full significance of the coming of the Christ. They must not despise these contemporary prophecies, since they come as inspired from the Lord.

But what then is the meaning of the admonition that they are to 'test everything'? What are they to test if the prophet's words are inspired of God? Does not this admonition presuppose that these new covenant prophecies involve a mixture of the good and the bad? The experience of God's people under the old covenant would point in another direction. It was normal procedure for the words of a prophet to be tested. It needed to be ascertained that the prophet spoke in accord with previous revelations (*Deut.* 13:1-5; 18:21-22). Only then could his word be regarded as authoritative for the people of God.

The counter-proposal is that under the old covenant only the prophet himself was to be tested, not his message (p. 105f.). Therefore this new covenant admonition presupposes a new kind of prophecy, a legitimate prophecy that must be tested because it contains a mixture of good and bad, of truth and error. But the suggestion that under the old covenant only the prophet's person was tested, not his message, contradicts the explicit instructions of the Lord to Israel: 'If what a prophet proclaims in the name of the Lord does not take place or come true, that is a message the Lord has not spoken' (*Deut.* 18:22). The book of Deuteronomy even goes so far as to envisage a case in which the word of the prophet comes to pass, but his message also includes a contradiction of the teaching of Scripture (*Deut.* 13:1-3). The total message is to be rejected, not merely the portion found to be in error, since any error in a prophecy indicates that the prophet has spoken presumptuously.

It may be suggested that the case has not been made for a completely new category of prophecy in the new covenant era, prophecy that is legitimate even though it mixes truth with error. The distinction between an infallible, foundational 'apostolic prophecy' and a legitimate 'ordinary congregational prophecy' that is both fallible and based on divine revelation has little basis in the evidence of Scripture. Rather, there is good reason to repeat our assertion that the hypothesis that the new covenant documents present a kind of prophecy that differs from old covenant prophecy hangs on an exegetical string. Neither in Corinthians nor in Acts nor in the other epistles of Paul does adequate evidence support this proposal. Prophecy in the new covenant age is linked directly with the same phenomena of revelation that occurred under the old covenant. Peter's indicator on the day of Pentecost establishes the line of continuity from old covenant prophecy to the new. Little evidence in the documents of the new covenant supports the rupture of that connection. No adequate basis may be found in the documents of the new covenant that would sanction a special kind of 'prophecy' in the worship services of the church that originates in a revelation from God but is mixed with error as it is delivered.

3. THIS VIEWPOINT BRINGS A VENERABLE INSTITUTION WITH AN IMPECCABLE HISTORY INTO A STATE OF DISREPUTE.

The new position on new covenant prophecy currently being considered has set for itself an unenviable task. It must establish that 'ordinary congregational' New Testament prophecy contains errors that keep it from having binding authority in the life of God's people.

Why must this viewpoint establish error in 'ordinary congregational' New Testament prophecy? It must establish this point because the whole intent of the position is to merge the strength of the *sola scriptura* position of the Protestant Reformation with the vitality associated with the modern Pentecostal movement. On the one hand, the intent is to affirm that the Bible and the Bible alone is the source of an authoritative word from the Lord. On the other hand, the desire is to capture the sense of freshness and liveliness in worship that comes from the experience of God's speaking right here and now to the people of God about their current problems through a revelational experience.

To its credit, this position does not fall into the trap of

shallow thinking which might propose that an inerrant word coming through a prophet today would not challenge the uniqueness of the authority of Scripture. Obviously a contemporary word from God with full divine authority would rival the functioning authority of Scripture in the lives of God's people. Addressing the concrete situation of believers and churches today, a contemporary divine word, infallible and inerrant in its nature, would certainly have greater impact on the life of God's people than the more general maxims of Scripture. If a contemporary prophetic word with full divine authority states that John should marry Martha, the couple would have no choice but to wed. The general scriptural maxims about marriage would be superseded by the more specific command, just as when Hosea the prophet was commanded to marry a woman who was a harlot (*Hos.* 1:2-3). The prophet had no choice but to follow exactly the word of the Lord.

To contend that a contemporary prophetic revelation would not rival the Bible so long as it was not actually added to the written canon of Scripture is to overlook the greater force of a direct word from the Lord addressing a particular issue than a general truth found in Scripture which must be applied to life by the believer. An illustration may help to clarify this point. A person may be preparing to teach a Sunday School lesson. He glances out of his window and sees his neighbour across the street sitting on his porch steps. Should he leave his lesson preparation and go visit with his neighbour, being sensitive to an opportunity to share the gospel? Or should he continue to work diligently at his studies in order to be fully prepared for his teaching responsibilities? As it stands at this point, the man is free to choose between these 'goods'. He can pray to God for wisdom, and then decide what he ought to do. But if a friend enters the room with a direct word from the Lord, then the man must listen with a commitment to obey. If the 'prophet' communicates God's word that he should leave his study and share the gospel with his neighbour right at that moment, he has no choice. The specific command from the Lord would have more concrete control over his life at that particular point than any general scriptural admonitions.

To its credit, the position currently being considered understands this principle. The clear desire is to acknowledge the unique authority of the Scriptures as the very word of God, and to offer no rival. But in order to maintain the unique authority of Scripture, this position must posit a kind of 'ordinary congregational prophecy' that is less than the very word of God, even though it originates with a direct revelation from God. So the effort must be made to find in Scripture a pattern of error in authentic prophetic words of the New Testament that could provide justification for the idea of an authentic prophetic word today that was not infallible and inerrant in its nature.

All through the ages of the old covenant the prophetic institution served the people of God with distinction as the principal instrument by which the revelation of God was communicated to his people. It was not just a matter of the prophet's receiving a revelation; it was that the prophet could be trusted to deliver to the people the perfected word of God. The words he spoke were God's words. The truth the people received from his mouth was nothing less than the very word of God. As the writer to the Hebrews underscores, it was 'through the prophets' that God spoke to the fathers (*Heb.* 1:1). They were the way of divine communication. The prophet's 'forth-speaking' defined the nature of revelational experience for God's people. It was not primarily the reception of the revelation by the prophet, but his delivery of the inspired, infallible and inerrant message from God that defined the nature of revelational experience for God's people.

Now comes this new proposal. The revelational dimension of the prophetic experience under the new covenant, it is proposed, must be restricted to the reception of the revelation by the prophet. His delivery of the revelation is clouded by human fallibilities. Several contemporary Pentecostal expressions on this matter are quoted with approval to make this point plain:

'Prophecy can be impure — our own thoughts or ideas can get mixed into the message we receive...'

'...there can be a whole range of degrees of inspiration, from the very high to the very low...'

'...one manifestation may be 75% God, but 25% the person's own thoughts...'

'A person may hear the voice of the Lord and be compelled to speak, but there is no assurance that it is pollutant-free. There will be a mixture of flesh and Spirit' (Grudem, pp. 110f.).

This cannot be a very happy position for an evangelical Christian to be found promoting. Certainly it clashes dissonantly with every concept of true prophecy as depicted in the old covenant Scriptures. Prophecy that can be characterized as impure, polluted, of the flesh, very low in inspiration, 75% God's, is not a very appealing phenomenon. Assuming a particular prophetic utterance passes the principal test and is not found to be contrary to the teaching of Scripture, how is it to be determined which part is pure and untainted with sin and which part impure, polluted and of the flesh? Would it not take a gift of revelational discernment to determine which portions of the prophecy were the very word of God?

This viewpoint is not in a very enviable position. It denigrates a very ancient institution of the Lord. It is in the peculiar position of elevating the experience of the old covenant saints above the experience of saints under the new covenant today.

4. THIS VIEWPOINT INTRODUCES A FACTOR OF UNCERTAINTY INTO WORSHIP

It would be better if the alleged 'prophetic' words could be regarded merely as the opinions of men. Then they might be discarded with a comfortable conscience. But if a prophetic utterance is based on a current revelation from God directed specifically to an individual or a church, how can it be relegated to a mere expression of human opinion? If 75% or more of the prophetic utterance is an accurate representation of a divine revelation, then it becomes the obligation of the hearers to determine what it is that God is saying, and then to do his revealed will without question or hesitation.

Yet the ambiguity remains.

So what impact will this ambiguity have on the Christian's peace of mind? Can a person's conscience remain guilt-free when he deliberately chooses to disobey a prophetic declaration addressed specifically to him, knowing that the prophet's directions very likely are based on a revelation from God about his concrete situation? It is neither a happy nor a healthy situation.

5. THIS VIEWPOINT HAS THE POTENTIAL OF BRINGING INTO QUESTION OTHER PROPHETIC REVELATIONS FROM GOD.

Obviously the current proponents of this view would affirm that this possibility is the furthest thing from their minds. But a teacher is merely a pointer for his pupils. It is the next generation that invariably discovers and develops the tangent of its teacher. The potential for deviation from a commitment to the full authority of Scripture must be noted with care. Affirming the erroneous character of 'congregational prophecy' in the New Testament is only a short step removed from affirming the presence of the same characteristics of fallibility in the prophecy of the old covenant Scriptures.

As has been noted, the view we are considering takes some pains to establish that the prophecies recorded in the book of Acts contain truth mixed with error. Because it is not explicitly confirmed that the Jews 'bound' Paul or 'handed him over' to the Romans, it is concluded that Agabus' prophecy is in error (pp. 96f.). But it would not be very difficult to 'discover' the same kind of 'errors' in the prophecies of the old covenant Scriptures. Even the predictions of Jesus himself could be found to contain this same kind of 'error'. Already the seeming discrepancy of Isaiah 53:9 has been noted. In another instance, Matthew states that Herod's slaughter of the infants of Bethlehem fulfilled the prophecy of Jeremiah: 'A voice is heard in Ramah ... Rachel weeping for her children' (*Matt.* 2:17-18, *Jer.* 31:15). Ramah is a little town about five miles north of Jerusalem, while Bethlehem is five miles south. Could it not then be suggested that the prophecy of Jeremiah was slightly in error? He prophesies that the weeping is to be done in Ramah, but it actually occurs in Bethlehem. Does not this discrepancy represent an error either in the prophecy of Jeremiah or in the application of Matthew? Again, Jesus prophesies that not one stone of the temple will be left on another (*Luke* 21:6). Yet anyone who has seen the wailing wall in Jerusalem knows that some stones still remain one on another. Again, Paul says the prophecy concerning the Messiah's giving of gifts to men is fulfilled by the outpouring of the Holy Spirit (*Eph.* 4:8). Yet the prophecy cited by Paul actually states that the Messiah 'received' gifts from men (*Ps.* 68:18). Obviously receiving gifts from men is the exact opposite of giving gifts to men. Is it therefore to be concluded that the psalmist made an error in his prophecy? Are we now forced to conclude that prophecies of the old covenant Scriptures involve a mixture of truth and error just as the congregational prophecies of the new covenant community are proposed to have contained? Must we now acknowledge that all of Scripture involves this confusion of flesh and Spirit, of truth and error?

The intent of the previous remarks is by no means to establish error in biblical prophecies. All of the supposed discrepancies between prophecy and fulfilment can be readily explained, just as the apparent discrepancies in the prophecy of Agabus can be explained. Grief over the tragic suffering of the chosen seed of God is the important thing in Jeremiah's prophecy, not the precise location of the weeping. In common human parlance, 'not one stone left upon another' need not mean absolutely not a single stone in contact with another. The 'receiving' of gifts by the Messiah is an Old Testament image of the homage of nations, and the 'giving' of gifts is simply a transformation of the imagery that underscores the gracious generosity that characterizes Messiah's kingdom. He 'receives' gifts only for the purpose of bestowing them.

But hopefully the dangers of this new position about prophecy have been made evident. Once this mindset of seeking error in the prophecies of Scripture is assumed, the old covenant prophecies will appear to be not materially different from new covenant prophecies. Let these illustrations suffice to indicate that promoting a view of new covenant prophecy that presumes to discover error mixed with truth is not an enviable position for an evangelical Christian. Once that position has been taken, the same mixture of truth and error may be found in all of prophecy, even in Scripture itself. As a matter of fact, one particular remark inadvertently acknowledges the likelihood of this conclusion. 'Indeed,' it is stated, 'there would seem to be some difficulty with holding to biblical inerrancy' if there were examples of the non-fulfilment of the details of Old Testament prophecy as in the cases of New Testament prophecy (p. 318, n. 37). This remark acknowledges that if the kinds of discrepancies that were found in the prophecies of Agabus also were discovered in Old Testament prophecies, then it would be difficult to continue holding to the inerrancy of the Bible. Yet the kind of precisionism displayed in the treatment of the prophecy of Agabus inevitably would find similar discrepancies in the fulfilment of Old Testament prophecies, as has been illustrated.

It is an unenviable position. It is an approach to prophecy that is bound to create serious difficulties, particularly for the evangelical Christian.

Chapter Five

Conclusion

It may be helpful to get a broader perspective on this entire issue by comparing the 'pros' and 'cons' of the two competing views on prophecy. The intention by this approach is not to locate the determining factor in this debate in pragmatic as over against exegetical considerations. Instead, the point is to look at the fruit that may be produced by the alternative views on prophecy and to assess their worth in terms of the health that may be provided for the people of God.

* * * * * * * *

Consider the consequences in the life of God's people that may flow from recognizing the continuation of 'ordinary congregational prophecy' based on fresh revelations of the Spirit today. Although these continuing prophecies may not be characterized by the perfections of old covenant prophecy, they would represent a word from the Lord addressed directly to a contemporary situation. Some would see a positive development in this perspective because the sons of the Protestant Reformation, affirming that 'Scripture alone' is the source of divine revelation, would discover a new basis for rapport with adherents of the modern Pentecostal movement. The solidarity of theological foundations thus would be joined with the vitality of modern-day Pentecostalism. In addition, some would see hope of ecclesiastical renewal in the breaking away from the old sterile mould that has restricted the expressiveness of contemporary Protestantism. New life might be breathed into the church by the meaningful participation of men, women and children in worship services through their exercise of the prophetic gift.

These are some of the positive factors that might be proposed as coming to the church through the recognition of the continuing gift of prophecy in the church. But there is a price to be paid for these proposed advances.

First of all, there is inevitably the denigration of the gift of prophecy. Rather than being seen exclusively as a unique, foundational gift essential for the communication of divine revelation to the church, prophecy has become something less than preaching, communicating a message that can be ignored even when it is directed to a specific personal or ecclesiastical situation.

Secondly, a minimizing of the vital role of Scripture in the life of the individual would appear to be the inevitable result of a recognition of the validity of this kind of new covenant prophecy. Without question the proponents of this viewpoint would deny this effect most vigorously. But by this view the church would be encouraged to look constantly for a fresh, vital word coming directly by revelation from the Lord and addressing the specific situation of the very moment. How could this expectation fail to reduce the role of Scripture in providing concrete direction for the life of God's people? For the specific word of the moment would take on greater significance than the general maxims of Scripture.

Thirdly, the consequential loss of the freedom of the Christian must be recognized. To the degree that a 'prophetic utterance' addresses the concrete circumstances of an individual, to that degree a person has lost the right to decide the course of life for himself in the light of his own conscience as instructed by the word of God. In those areas of a person's life where a prophetic utterance had spoken, responsible decision-making would be replaced by an effort to determine which part of the supposed word from the Lord was to him the very word of God, and which part had been polluted by the sinful flesh of the prophetic messenger.

Fourthly, the potential for stifling healthy growth in Christ must be recognized. The reason for Paul's having to deal so extensively with the gifts of the Spirit was the immaturity of the Corinthian Christians. Their concentration on the gifts indicated that they had not yet comprehended the superiority of graces over gifts. Paul tells them that their aspiration should be to see the grace of love as more important than all the gifts. Indeed, he encourages them in their experience of the gift of prophecy; but he does so with the insistence that they move toward the putting away of childish things for the superior gift of love.

It may be supposed that some advantages would come from the introduction of this new kind of fallible, ordinary congregational prophecy into the life of the church. But the results would appear to fall far more on the negative than on the positive side. As a matter of fact, even the supposed gains from adopting this position may prove to represent losses in the end.

* * * * * * * *

Let us now consider the advantages and disadvantages of the view which affirms that Christ and the revelations associated with his coming are 'the final word'. According to this view, no further special revelations from God are expected until Christ returns in glory.

Negatively, it might be proposed that holding this position closes a person off from the continuing activities of revelation that could provide many blessings to the church today. The staleness, the formality, the lack of spontaneity and life would be perpetuated because there would be no expectation that God would speak directly by new revelations of the Spirit. It also could be proposed that denying any possibility of God's speaking directly to someone in the present day appears to be rather presumptuous. Who has the right to limit God, to say that he cannot speak by special revelation if he chooses to do so? Furthermore, it might be suggested that no clear teaching in Scripture declares that the gifts of prophecy and tongues have ceased. Apart from some specific statements in this regard, should it not be assumed that all the gifts of the Spirit continue in the church today? The force of these arguments should be felt. It certainly is not proper for anyone to presume to limit God, building on an assumption that may not be stated explicitly in Scripture.

Hopefully the previous discussion of these very considerations has some relevance to these points. Obviously it is not within the power of any human being to limit God. In any case, who would want to limit the activity of the Almighty? At the same time, consistency is a major attribute of the personhood of God. The Lord has established a pattern over the millennia in which advancements in special revelation are coordinated with advancements in the accomplishment of redemption. For this reason, it can be expected that the historical completion of the work of redemption by Christ in his death and resurrection will be accompanied by a rounding out of revelation as the significance of those events is fully interpreted. If certain offices and functions such as apostle and prophet are treated in Scripture as foundational for the establishment of the church, it should come as no surprise that the extraordinary gifts associated with these offices should cease once the historical foundation of the church has been laid.

In making these affirmations, it is not so much a matter of limiting God as it is giving expression to the expectation that he will act in consistency with himself. Generally people of an evangelical persuasion would have no trouble affirming that the sufferings of Christ have ended. He suffered once and for all. He will not return to earth again in humility. He will not be required to experience rejection, crucifixion and the curse of God a second time. In a similar way, it should not be expected that he will be resurrected and ascend to heaven in order to begin his session at the right hand of the Father a second time. These events by their very nature have a distinctive place in redemptive history that do not come around again. It is not so much limiting God by affirming that he will not have Christ crucified, raised and lifted to heaven over and over again. Instead, it is simply acknowledging the once-for-all character of these events in the progress of redemptive history.

The confirmation of the Spirit's outpouring by the manifestation of certain extraordinary gifts and offices falls into this same category of redemptive events. The offices of apostle and prophet will not keep popping up in the experience of the church. These offices and their associated gifts were essential for laying the foundation of the new covenant church. They were required for the establishment of the church, but not for its perpetual maintenance. Except as the authority of these offices and gifts are retained through Scripture for the church's stability, their continuation is unnecessary for the life of God's people.

On the positive side, the many benefits associated with the finality of revelation as it is found in Christ and the completed Scripture are often overlooked. Affirming the end of revelation is not principally negative in its orientation. Instead, it is a positive statement by which the church affirms that the work of redemption has reached its goal in so far as this age is concerned by the coming of Christ. Even as the faith of the church and the joy of its life are enhanced by the affirmation that Christ never will be sacrificed again, so the church's faith and joy are multiplied when it is affirmed that the 'final word' has been spoken, that God has delivered all the information that is needed for the life of his church, and that the way to fullness of life and godliness throughout this age can be found in the Scriptures. Consider just a few of the blessings that come as a consequence of affirming a finalized revelation in the Scriptures:

Firstly, a new appreciation of the wonders of God's working in everyday providences will be perceived more clearly. People who are looking for the spectacular or the extraordinary become distracted so that they do not always see how great is the way God orders ordinary processes to meet the needs of his people. As Jesus said, it is an evil and adulterous generation that continually looks for a new miraculous sign (*Matt.* 12:39, *Luke* 11:29). Far more mature is the faith that sees God's hand of providence working in the Lord's daily ordering of life than a faith that depends on constantly seeing the spectacular.

Secondly, more attention will be placed on the wondrous working of God in regeneration. How can an act of the miraculous healing of the body compare with the wonder of the new birth? Which is more spectacular, a supposed occasional word of new revelation to an individual, or the opening of the ears of the spiritually deaf so that they actually hear and heed the life-giving words of the preached word? Understanding that new revelations of the Spirit occur no more will enable the church to concentrate its attention on the newness of life being imparted by the risen Christ.

Thirdly, greater attention will be directed toward a full comprehension of the words of the Bible by use of the ordinary means of grace. Rather than looking for spectacular communications that might come through new prophetic revelations as the source of truth to solve life's difficult problems, the people of God will pay much closer attention to the private reading and public preaching of the word of God. As they listen more attentively to that word, proclaimed clearly and authoritatively by ministers gifted by God and filled with the Spirit, they will mature in the faith, receive guidance for their lives, and be enabled to serve others in the spirit of Christ. The people of God also will come to appreciate more fully the sacraments as the means of grace by which visible signs ordained by Christ confirm them in their faith. Rather than looking for a miraculous sign from God to give them direction for their lives, the symbol of his broken body will confirm the fact that God continues to bless them in their successes and despite their sins, for 'he that spared not his own Son, but delivered him up for us all, how shall he not with him also freely give us all things?' (*Rom.* 8:32).

Acceptance of the fact that the final revelation has been given will invariably deepen the church's commitment to the ordinary means of grace. It is in this way that God has promised to meet all the needs of his people. Instead of constantly searching for some new confirmation of God's grace in the present distress through signs, wonders, prophecies and revelations, the church will find its unshakeable stability in the faith once delivered to the saints.

Fourthly, responsible adulthood among the saints of God will be realized much more quickly when it is understood that with Christ comes a new freedom to be energetically creative in serving the Lord. The Christian is not bound to wait for some special word from God before he attempts great things in service to the Lord. The promises and challenges of Scripture are enough. With prayer, the Spirit, and wisdom from above in assessing gifts and resources, the Christian is freed to attempt great things for God, expecting great things from God. Too long the church has been crippled in its creative efforts to serve Christ because it has been waiting for a 'sign' or a 'revelation' that might come in one way or another to tell them what to do. But if it is understood that all the knowledge of God's will that is needed to confirm them in a contemplated act of service is found in Scripture, then the pent-up energies of God's people will be released with power.

In sum, great benefits come to God's people if they are willing to take seriously the fact that the 'final revelation' has come in the Christ of the Scriptures. Far from hindering enthusiasm and a sense of the immediacy of God's presence in their midst, faith in the sufficiency of Scripture will move them to serve him with the full vigour of their beings. It must not be forgotten how the resurrected Christ stirred the hearts of his depressed disciples. The Gospel of Luke explains that Jesus enlivened his followers by opening to them the Scriptures. Beginning with Moses and all the prophets, he explained to them what was said in all the scriptures concerning himself (*Luke* 24:27). Why? Why did the resurrected Christ speak to them in this way? Why did he not simply give to them a new revelation?

The resurrected Jesus opened the scriptures to them because that would be the way by which spiritual life would be sustained for them from that point on. As a consequence of his opening the Scriptures, their hearts burned within them (*Luke* 24:32). The same principle has continued through all the ages. As the resurrected Christ through his Spirit opens the Scriptures to his people, their hearts have burned within them. Much greater than depending on the stimulus of new revelations of the Spirit is living out of the sufficiency of the final word as it is found in the Christ of the Scriptures.

And why not both? Why not the illumination of Scripture coupled with new revelations of the Spirit? Simply because if you declare a need for both, you have implied the insufficiency of the one. You have placed yourself back in the framework of the old covenant, in a time when new revelations were required because of the incompleteness of the old. But Christ is the final word. No further word for the redemption of men in the present age is needed. In Scripture is found all the truth that is needed for life and godliness.

May the Lord grant to his church today a full unleashing of its potential that comes from the full knowledge of the truth as it is found in Jesus. For he is the final word.

Notes

Chapter 1

1. Geerhardus Vos, 'The Idea of "Fulfilment" of Prophecy in the Gospels', in Richard B. Gaffin, ed., *Redemptive History and Biblical Interpretation*, Phillipsburg, N.J., 1980, p.354.
2. Benjamin Breckenridge Warfield, 'The Biblical Idea of Revelation', in *Revelation and Inspiration*, Grand Rapids, 1981 reprint, p.23.

Chapter 3

1. The author acknowledges the insights gained from Jonathan Edwards' *Charity and its Fruits*, a series of messages first preached to his congregation in Northampton in 1738. See the edition published by The Banner of Truth, Edinburgh, 1969, pp.317f.
2. See H.N. Ridderbos, *The Speeches of Peter in the Acts of the Apostles*, Tyndale Press, London, 1961.
3. *Catechism for Young Children*, Great Commission Publications, Philadelphia, Question 13.
4. It was William Carey's apprehension of this fact which lay at the foundation of the missionary movement as it originated in the English-speaking world. See Carey's *Enquiry* (Leicester, 1792), reprinted in Timothy George, *Faithful Witness: The Life and Mission of William Carey*, IVP, Leicester, 1992.

Chapter 4

1. Wayne Grudem, *The Gift of Prophecy in the New Testament and Today*, Kingsway Publications, Eastbourne, 1988.
2. Johannes Munck (in *The Acts of the Apostles*, Doubleday & Co., Garden City, New York, 1967, p.207) makes a sensible distinction between the urgings of the congregation and the Holy Spirit's prediction: 'During his visit there, Paul got in touch with the local congregation which urged him not to go up to Jerusalem because of

the Holy Spirit's prediction that his life would be imperilled there.'

F. F. Bruce (in *Commentary on the Book of the Acts*, Wm. B. Eerdmans Publishing Co., Grand Rapids, 1979, p.421) states in a similar vein: 'It was natural that his friends who by the prophetic spirit were able to foretell his tribulation and imprisonment should try to dissuade him from going on...'

See also J. A. Alexander, *Commentary on the Acts of the Apostles*, Zondervan Publishing House, Grand Rapids, 1956 reprint, p.722: 'This was not a divine command to Paul, but an inference of the disciples from the fact, which was revealed to them, that Paul would there be in great danger.'

A full recognition of the problem and a sensible solution can also be found in John Calvin, *Commentary upon the Acts of the Apostles*, Baker Book House, Grand Rapids, 1984, vol. II, p.268.

Index of Names and Subjects

In the index the following abbreviations have been used:
N.T.—New Testament, O.C.—Old Covenant, O.T.—Old Testament, n—note.

and tongues, 28

Grudem, Wayne
advocacy of continuing
revelation, 85-126
Scriptural arguments
answered, 98-119
and reception of revela-
tion, 87
*The Gift of Prophecy in the
New Testament and
Today*, 86, 137n

Hebrews, letter to, and the
finality of revelation, 5
Holy Spirit
and Agabus' predictions,
109, 111-12
descends on Gentiles, 72
and erroneous prophecy,
112-13
gifts
—their cessation, 67-78
—their purpose, 37-8, 39
illumination of Scripture,
55-60
inspiration of Scripture,
59
and interpretation of
tongues, 33
in Joel's prophecy, 11-12
and prophecy 11-12, 14,
15, 88
and the seventy elders in
the wilderness, 64
signs in Samaria, 72
and tongues, 34
Hosea, commanded to

marry a harlot, 120
Human fallibility, and
prophecy, 88, 90-3, 96-7
Insight, not the same as 'a
word from God', 55-6
Isaiah, prophecy about
foreign tongues, 43-45

Jeremiah
on false prophets, 8
prophecy concerning
foreign tongues, 46
Jerusalem, tongues 72; *see
also* Pentecost
Jesus Christ
the climax of revelation,
53-6, 59, 67-70
and the finality of pro-
phetic revelation 5, 11,
131-5
the prophetic mediator,
10-11
many signs unrecorded,
57
many words unrecorded,
58
Joel, and prophecy, 11-13,
20, 43, 106-7
John, in Samaria, 72

Law
ceremonial law no longer
binding, 79-80
dietary laws no longer
binding, 79-80
and God's revealed will,
3; *see also* Sinai

Index of Scripture References

There is one instance in the text where a Scripture is alluded to without a Scripture reference being given. That reference has been supplied in this index with the addition of an asterisk to show that chapter and verse are not cited on the page indicated.

SOME OTHER
BANNER OF TRUTH
TITLES

Another title by the same author:

JONAH
A Study in Compassion

The Old Testament story catches the imagination and tells of a prophet who disobeys God and of a great fish which can swallow a man; it describes a city-wide revolt in a pagan country and a wonderfully-sighted prophet sulking in the sunshine. What does it mean?

In *Jonah: A Study in Compassion*, Dr O. Palmer Robertson's masterly knowledge of the Hebrew language, his vivid sense of the grace of God and the twisted state of a man's heart, and his ability to retell historical events and see their significance all combine to explain what the message of the book of Jonah really is, and—since there is a string in the tail—what it really means for us today.

ISBN 0 85151 575 4
64pp. Paperback

BIBLICAL THEOLOGY
Old and New Testaments
Geerhardus Vos

The aim of this book is no less than to provide an account of the unfolding of the mind of God in history, through the successive agents of his special revelation. Vos handles this under three main divisions: the Mosaic epoch of revelation, the prophetic epoch of revelation, and the New Testament.

Such an historical approach is not meant to supplant the work of the systematic theologian; nevertheless, the Christian gospel is inextricably bound up with history, and the biblical theologian thus seeks to highlight the uniqueness of each biblical document in that succession. The rich variety of Scripture is discovered anew as the progressive development of biblical themes is explicated.

To read these pages—the fruit of Vos' 39 years of teaching biblical theology at Princeton—is to appreciate the late John Murray's suggestion that Geerhardus Vos was the most incisive exegete in the English-speaking world of the twentieth century.

Geerhardus Vos was born in the Netherlands, emigrating to the United States in 1881 at the age of 19. In 1893 he was invited to Princeton Seminary, where he had studied, to teach biblical theology. He remained there until his retirement in 1932. He died in 1949.

ISBN 0 85151 458 8
440pp Large Paperback